MEN

ON DIVORCE

The Other Side of the Story

MEN ON

The Other

DIVORCE

Side of the Story

EDITED BY *Penny Kaganoff*

AND *Susan Spano*

A HARVEST BOOK

HARCOURT BRACE & COMPANY

San Diego   New York   London

Library of Congress Cataloging-in-Publication Data
Men on divorce: the other side of the story/edited by Penny
Kaganoff and Susan Spano.
p. cm.
ISBN 0-15-100115-4   ISBN 0-15-600547-6 (pbk.)
1. Divorced men—United States—Psychology. 2. Divorced men—
United States—Attitudes. 3. Divorce—United States—Psychological
aspects. I. Kaganoff, Penny. II. Spano, Susan.
HQ834.M45 1997   306.89–DC21 96-50302

Text set in Galliard   Designed by Camilla Filancia
Printed in the United States of America   First Harvest edition 1998
F E D C B A

With love for

ALETA KAGANOFF

RONI & ELI GREENBAUM

LEANA, CHAI, SHELI & BETSY GREENBAUM

and for

MARTHA & SCOTT HARRIS

CONTENTS

We are especially grateful to Walt Bode
and Theo Lieber for their editorial wizardry.

Special thanks also go to Lisa Bankoff,
Ruth Greenstein, Irene Reichbach, Claire Wachtel,
Dori Weintraub, Linda Yellin, our loving parents,
and to sundry friends, colleagues, and relatives
for their kindnesses to us during the creation
of this book.

INTRODUCTION

THE IDEA for this book came about in the fall of 1993, when we first met at a restaurant in New York City. A friend had brought us together because she knew we were both writers and thought we had something else in common, as well. Susan was in the midst of a divorce, while Penny's papers had come through several years before. We talked steadily through lunch and into the late afternoon about books and publishing. But eventually, the conversation turned to personal matters, above all, our divorces. We learned that we had different reasons for ending our marriages and different perspectives. But the experience had been awful for us both, tearing apart our lives, changing the way we saw ourselves and others, and forcing us to reevaluate some of our most cherished beliefs. It also had left us with identical questions: What causes divorce? What would a good relationship be like?

And what does it take, these days, to make a marriage last?

To answer these questions—both for ourselves and for all the other men and women who are currently undergoing the pain of divorce or are looking back trying to make sense of it all—we compiled *Women on Divorce: A Bedside Companion,* adding our divorce experiences to those of twelve women writers. In their essays, we found divergences, shared themes, astonishing revelations, reasons for hope and despair, compelling stories—but perhaps best of all, fascinating minds at work, grappling with the problem of failed marriage.

Of course, divorce is like a novel with (at least) two points of view. So even as we embarked upon the women's volume, we knew there were other questions our female contributors simply couldn't hope to answer: What do men think about divorce? What is their side of the story?

Given our personal experiences, we approached these questions with certain assumptions, to be sure. But ours were the assumptions of the culture at large, which has tended to view divorced men in stereotypical fashion— as midlife crisis victims, absent husbands and fathers, unbearable abusers, inveterate playboys. Clearly, there had to be more to it than this, something more complex and challenging. As well, we wondered whether the men's side of the divorce story would ever align with that of the women—and if so, how?

So we set about compiling a companion volume to *Women on Divorce: A Bedside Companion.* In this effort we were greatly aided by our editor, Walt Bode, and his assistant editor, Theo Lieber, who provided a male perspective, urged us to seek the broadest possible spectrum of men's views, and often led us to a deeper, more fully sympathetic understanding of what our male essayists were saying. They were our gender bridges, and for that we are very grateful.

The fifteen writers included in *Men on Divorce: The Other Side of the Story* come from culturally and ethnically diverse backgrounds and have been touched by divorce in widely different ways—from the quickie Mexican variety, so prevalent in the years before divorce laws were eased, to separations that last for decades, leaving both spouses free in fact, if not by law. Some of the essayists discuss marriages that ended long ago and are therefore able to look back with the wisdom of age, while others write about divorces that are more recent —and raw. A number of the contributors make assessments and judgments; or in attempting to answer the questions we put to them, only raise more compelling questions; or simply tell involving fragments of divorce stories, leaving readers to judge for themselves. There are marriages described here that clearly had to end; divorces regretted; portraits of "bad-boy" runarounds and deeply devoted husbands and fathers—which occasionally co-exist in the same essay, and man.

And some of the themes treated by the men in this collection align perfectly with those explored by the women writers in the companion volume. Chief among these is the idea that divorce is often driven by patterns in a family background or by the divorce of a person's parents, which reaches out, as Walter Kirn puts it in "My Parents' Bust-Up. And Mine" like a "long, branching crack." His mother and father waited until he was grown-up and married himself before announcing they were getting a divorce. But when the blow eventually landed it was no less shattering, sapping him of the faith and optimism marriage requires, and ultimately leading to his own divorce.

In "Pandora's Box," happily married Jonathan Rosen recalls learning at age thirteen that there had been a divorce in his mother's past, which at once fascinated him and made him feel betrayed. Like some juvenile sleuth, he embarked on a quest to find out about the man who "might have been my father," with only limited success. Perhaps as a result, that man remains a frightening phantom in his life to the present day—making him constantly aware of the fragility of even a happy marriage, which "ends inevitably in the terrible divorce of death."

Looking back on a young, unhappy union in "Guns & Love," Benjamin Cheever comes to understand why he got married in the first place. "My father was so busy killing himself. His doctor had told him many times that if he didn't stop drinking, he'd die. He didn't stop drinking." He sees that his ex-wife had family-linked reasons for making a disastrous marriage, as well. Do "not marry a woman who doesn't like her father, even, and especially, if she says you're so different from the old man. Someday she'll stop making the distinction, and she'll hate you every bit as well as she has hated him."

Back then, Cheever married to the strains of the Lettermen singing "that when they fell in love, it would be forever"—and thus labored under a romantic illusion that seems to have doomed the relationship to failure. In the same way, romanticizing marriage and idealizing a spouse caused a long train of relationships to derail in Luis Rodriguez's life (though for Rodriguez, the son of poor Mexican immigrants, there were added socioeconomic obstacles, as well). Mourning the end of one such relationship, he suddenly realized that he'd turned the woman involved into a "figment of my imagination." "I didn't miss . . . the real person," he writes in "A Heart Gone Mad: One Man's Tale of Love and Divorce." "I missed the dream."

The idealization theme arose in the women's volume, too, but not as persistently as in this collection. The danger in idealizing a spouse, as several of the male writers suggest, is that eventually the perfect image of the wife is bound to shatter, leaving the husband either ill-equipped or unready to face the reality behind the dream. In "Courtship Mode," Stephen Dobyns delves profoundly into what the urge to idealize is all about, suggesting that men and women both seek perfection in prospective mates as a kind of rejection of mortality. The facade free from imperfection promises "happiness forever after." "I once read that Cardinal Richelieu only liked kittens," he says. "When they reached adolescence he gave them away. And I ask myself what it was that kept me from reaching the adolescence—not even the adulthood—of any relationship."

Dobyns eventually met a woman who made him turn away from the charged but deluded chase for perfection. "She worked to keep the marriage going and taught me how to work on it, too." Nor is he the only writer in this book to come to a new understanding of what keeps a marriage going once the thrill of romance wears out. "Love is work. It's good work, if you can get it. But it's work nevertheless," Cheever writes.

In "Bedroom Tapestries," Tim Parks tells the chilling story of a man in the doldrums of marriage, who became possessed by a first affair. His lover seemed the very embodiment of eros, while his wife became "She Who Must Be Obeyed" and marital sex devolved into what Parks's friend called "duty-fucking." But as Parks makes stunningly clear, the man idealized his lover; and when he left his wife and family for her, chaos ensued—leading Parks to write: "Marriage and divorce are so tangled up with our sense of mortality. One lives such a short time, yet wishes to do everything. Then to recapture everything. Start again, the springtime says. Unfaithfulness never fails to rejuvenate. But if we start again too often, nothing will be brought to completion."

Many of the essays in this book describe lives filigreed with long chains of relationships, men who move serially from one woman to the next, repeating the same mistakes over the course of each involvement and arriving at the same failure. We rarely found this theme in *Women on Divorce: A Bedside Companion,* possibly due to the particular sampling of female writers included in that volume. Certainly its presence in this book occasionally caused the two of us to ruefully recall the stereotype of the skirt chaser. But then we listened more carefully as a number of the male essayists struggled to understand their lives, to break out of behavior patterns that had made their marriages and relationships fall apart.

Generally, it seemed to us and our male editors that many of the men were uncomfortable with the sort of emotionally intense self-examination common in the women's volume. But there are striking exceptions to this rule. In "Getting the Point," Ted Solotaroff admits that he had it easier than his ex-wives after their divorce; and more importantly, he explains why. "Getting on with it, putting the problem behind you, is what men are trained to do." But divorce "is not like a lost tennis match or business setback," he goes on to say. "What is needed is not to just do something but to sit there with the guilt and grief—to mourn and learn and begin to atone...."

Certainly, Michael Ventura, the author of "The Ex-Files," pursued this course of grief and self-examination—an experience so excoriating that it left him unwilling to make claims about any great lessons learned. But he does say that after enduring a long season of post-divorce despair, he has begun to see how he might attend to his life with dignity, "endure the lacks, relish the pleasures, and not spread the pain around too much."

However, not all lessons are learned through pain. Humor works as well, as we found in Michael Ryan's sharply observed and satirical "How to Get Divorced: A Practical Guide." Of course, men (and women, for that matter) would be well advised to turn around tips like "Never allow intercourse to result from tender feeling" if they're seriously interested in staying married.

In "Learning to Be Single," catharsis came for Lawrence Block, not through pain, but in a fit of laughter—aimed largely at himself. Suddenly, he understood why he had ricocheted from one relationship to another after his divorce. "I was always either in a relationship or between relationships," he wryly recalls. "I might be between relationships for months at a time, holding open auditions all the while, but that's not the same as being single." Ironically, he finally managed to create a happy, stable relationship with his present wife by first learning how to live with himself—in his own company and space.

Interestingly, instead of turning a magnifying glass on a failed marriage in order to analyze what went wrong (as so many of the women in our first collection did), a number of the male writers assess their divorces by taking a long step back and looking at their lives from a distance. From that perspective they are able to see larger, social and historical factors that played a part in their failed relationships and divorces. Growing up as a black American during the Depression, John Williams did not get the encouragement he needed to realize his desire to become a writer. "Food and rent always came first, and I understood that quite well. Writing was not work; it was for a few foolish white people." So, as he explains in "Ending Well," he got a job, and a wife—only to later leave her when his need for a different sort of life altogether, that of a writer, grew too great to deny.

Straitened circumstances and racial prejudice contributed to the divorces of others, as well—sparking destructive rages in Rodriguez and leaving Herb Boyd with no reason to stay in a young marriage, even after his daughter was born. "As a product of a broken home and surrounded by a host of friends with similar backgrounds, I had very little intimate knowledge of two-parent families with children," Boyd explains in "Unchained Malady."

For those who lived (and loved) through the fifties and sixties, Edward Hoagland's "Fidelities" should strike resounding chords. His essay looks back on the texture of his life in New York City during days of the Beat Generation when he married his first wife and lived with her in the East Village, and then moves on to the hippie era in the West Village, where he settled with his second wife. But he weighs his experience of two failed marriages against his parents' union, which lasted only because, in their day and social circle, divorce was anathema. "I can't imagine hating one's former spouse," he writes, "but people sometimes did when they couldn't get divorced. Singly, we're so much freer now. We can scarcely burn our bridges because we've got so few that matter."

To social and historical perspectives on divorce, this collection adds cross-cultural assessments. Indeed, in Parks's essay we find an Italian therapist explaining to a troubled, unfaithful husband that his problems stem from his Anglo-Saxon Puritan upbringing, which had led him to attach too much importance to his lover. And the prescription? "Take a few mild tranquilizers, settle down, and have another affair."

On the other side of the globe, Richard Gilman describes the rare Japanese divorce—an ossified, agonizing process, as he discovered while seeing the Japanese woman who is his present wife through the ordeal. She lost everything—above all her children—to an ex-husband whose monstrous vengefulness was largely condoned by the state. Still, in "The Sorrow and the Need," Gilman finds reason for sympathy with the man. "I don't have to like or respect him, and I certainly don't. But I have to respect the fact of his suffering."

But this Japanese ex-husband is not the only one to have suffered. Gilman also describes a variety of sadness that exists apart from the particulars of each divorce mess. It is "a sorrowfulness, a mourning for something lost, accompanied by slight feelings of wrongdoing and failure, and—so fugitive I have to strain to capture it— that old sense of broken taboo." He goes on to say that "Divorce is necessary at times, yes, of course, but it's a necessary evil, not an unalloyed good. That it *has to be* available is precisely the source of the sadness."

There is sadness aplenty at the end of "Banging the Ex," though at the start it seems as if rage and hormones might be in control as Daniel Asa Rose tells the sexy, funny, heartaching story of how he settled some unfinished business with his ex. But in his case, two beloved children figure at the center of the tale. In the women's volume the effects of divorce on children arose as a principal theme, while in this volume it generally only whispers through the essays—in mentions of sons and daughters who turned out all right despite their parents' splits or were lost to noncustodial ex-husbands in the aftermath of divorce. But Rose's sons bound him to his ex-wife, as the living products of a loving marriage, and later as the progeny of an acrimonious divorce. It is through their eyes that he sees the chaos and sadness loosed by divorce, as he drives away hearing them say, "Bye-bye, bye-bye, bye-bye."

That's divorce, in a word. There are many other ways to express it, of course, which, in the end, has perhaps been the whole purpose of this book and its predecessor. We hope that both volumes will not only stand as examples of wonderful essays by contemporary writers, but will help all those who have been divorced, are going through the terrible process, or are watching from the sidelines as someone they care about weathers the storm. And more specifically, we hope that *Men on Divorce: The Other Side of the Story* will help men better understand themselves, and women better understand men.

Penny Kaganoff
Susan Spano
NEW YORK CITY
September 1996

MEN

ON DIVORCE

The Other Side of the Story

GUNS & LOVE

BY *Benjamin H. Cheever*

LAST WINTER I saw her again. I'd gone into the Sawmill Multiplex early in the day to buy tickets for a sneak preview that night, and heading out and down the broad cement stairs, I came up behind them: the woman and her mother.

The new husband pulled up in a white Toyota. He had a beard. I'd heard he had a beard. He jumped out of the car to open doors for the women. The girl I had loved was holding a large wax-paper cup of some sort of soda, with the straw still in it. Diet soda, I'd bet.

I hadn't seen her for at least a decade. She looked good. Both frail and haughty. She always had that long, serious face. She might have been a judge, or a senator in Republican France. In college I met a man who told me she was the only girl he knew who could look dignified on a commode. "What is a commode?" I asked, and he told me, and I agreed.

This time she was wearing one of those white sheepskin coats where the fur is on the inside and at the cuffs. Her hair was gold, almost white. I heard her ask if her mother wanted to sit up front, with the husband. "Do you want to sit up front, Mom?" I think those were her words, although I wouldn't swear to it. If you want to know exactly, you'd better ask her. She never liked it when I reported on our life together, and I don't mean in writing, I mean in our living room. She didn't like her life coming out in my words. "It's my life," she used to say. "It's my body."

I don't know if they saw me and pretended not to, pretended I was dead, or if they simply didn't notice.

I didn't make a sound. I walked off to my car. My new and much beloved wife was in the passenger seat; both our boys were in the back. Probably they were making a racket. Usually they are making a racket.

I waited until I had backed out of the slot and had the car moving forward before I spoke.

"You'll never guess who I saw."

"Yes, I will."

"I saw Amy."

"I know. How did she look?"

I shrugged. "She looked good," I said, trying to keep my voice in the lower register.

Then my wife said, "You thought she was going to die."

And I said, "That's right. Maybe if I had stayed, she would have died."

IT WAS THAT sort of marriage. An illness, really, involving two adults and then one boy. It was an illness built around an ideal. An ideal we didn't even have to invent. Our concept of love was in the culture, it was on the radio, it was practically in the water we drank.

Remember the Lettermen? The LP I'm thinking of had a picture of these guys all standing around in their cardigan sweaters. They sang that when they fell in love, "bump, bump, bump," it would be forever, "bump, bump, bump." That's what I thought.

Now I wonder what exactly they meant by "forever." Probably they meant "forever, or at the very least until I get laid." Because that song, like a lot of the songs I grew up with, wasn't about love at all. It was about anticipation. It was about romance. And love is a different animal altogether. Love is work. It's good work, if you can get it. But it's work nevertheless.

This was just one of the facts I was not in possession of when I got married the first time. Come to think of it, there weren't many facts I was in possession of. I knew how to unfasten a brassiere with one hand. I was not an adept, though. I couldn't do it and talk.

I don't even know why we got married when we did. A friend and I were going to hitchhike across the country. We got as far as Ohio, and he called his girlfriend. She'd missed her period. We flew back to New York. She got her period, and I got married. To my girlfriend. Who had not missed her period. Go figure.

We did it in a hurry. We announced our intentions on a Tuesday and got married on a Thursday, two days later. Or maybe we announced our intentions on a Thursday and got married on a Tuesday. You might ask her. In any case, it was too fast. We were taking the law into our own hands. Everybody came; nobody approved.

The bride and I headed off on a new motorcycle. There was a dinner afterwards, for everybody else, and my father told my new mother-in-law that I was never going to amount to anything, but that it didn't matter, because he was loaded. He was loaded, all right. Full of gin. Although there wasn't a great deal of money.

Like most men, I thought that I'd married the woman I loved because she wanted to get married. And she did want to get married. I can see now that I must have been deeply influenced by the fact that my father was so busy killing himself. His doctor had told him many times that if he didn't stop drinking, he'd die. He didn't stop drinking. So I was trying to escape my father's illness. She might have been trying to escape her father. She was an only child. Her father had high expectations. Marrying me would settle his hash.

I don't have any very clear recollection of the ceremony, except that it didn't work. It wasn't serious enough to scare us away. Weddings should be frightening. Even dangerous. I've thought a lot about this. I have one good idea, which is that the man and the woman might each be given a revolver and temporary immunity from criminal charges. She gets in her gown, he gets in his tuxedo, and they stand about twelve feet apart. The man of God counts to three. At some weddings she'd shoot him in the heart. Sometimes he'd murder her. The idea, of course, would be to have them both discharge their weapons into the air. But I don't want a hollow ceremony. There would have to be an incentive for a killing. If she did nail the bastard, she'd get all his worldly goods. And if he had no worldly goods, he'd have to take out an insurance policy beforehand. Make it worth her while. And vice versa. Make it worth his while to kill her outright rather than to destroy her life by siege. Which seems to be the preferred method.

Not only would this cut down on the excess of unloved children, but it would also add the sort of excitement you don't ordinarily get at a wedding, no matter how gifted the caterer.

Love is both a destructive and a constructive passion, and I think it would be swell if we could settle at the get go which impulse was in the driver's seat.

DO I SOUND bitter? Well, I am. Because my first marriage was a car wreck. It was an imprisonment. And I know this because my second marriage has been a release, which I would not have thought possible. But what still astonishes me is how dramatically love can change a person. And how little motives have to do with the results. Because if my first wife and I had been given pistols, we would certainly have fired into the air.

It was ourselves we tried to hurt, not each other. I burned my arm with a lighted cigarette, banged my head into walls. She used to lock herself in the bathroom, take everything out of the medicine cabinet and throw it into the tub. *Smash, smash.* When I broke the door lock, she'd be swooning on the floor. Where the hell are the Lettermen now? I used to wonder.

When Hemingway's Robert Jordan slept with Maria in *For Whom the Bell Tolls* and the earth moved, many readers sighed with appreciation. He's one fine writer, of course, but the earth doesn't only shift when you're doing the deed, it moves permanently. Fall in love and everything changes. It's not just that there were birds all around, and you never heard them singing. It's much more global. Really fall in love and you might wake up a Young Republican, or a fascist, or on the action committee of the SDS. You can fall asleep with a girl in your arms and wake up to find that the world has turned away from the sun, away from light and life and every idle joy.

When I married my first wife, I moved in with her family. We could have moved in with my family, but she was an only child. My parents had other children. And also dogs. My parents were more interested in their own lives than ours. My parents weren't always happy to be interrupted. Whereas her parents seemed happy to be interrupted. They were always glad to see us. They were always glad to see her, anyway. And I was there. An undergraduate male. With hair down to his shoulders and a poet's slouch. Just what an IBM executive craves in his son-in-law.

I tried to fit in. Boy, did I try to fit in. I wasn't entirely successful. We were sitting on the patio one afternoon, and I was talking about some people whose taste was so bad that the toilet in their house was one color, the sink another. "Toilets should be white," I said. "Sinks should be white. Always have been. Always should be." There was a pause, and then my new mother-in-law pointed out that her sink was one color, her toilet another.

I don't remember now what I said. But it wasn't courageous. I was, after all, living in their house, with their precious daughter. I backpedaled. This much I recall. I did a lot of backpedaling over the decade of that first marriage.

Grill my ex-wife and she'd tell you that I wasn't actually so pliant. Although I did try. We both struggled with the romantic ideal. We used to coo at each other through clenched teeth.

She didn't trust me. And she was right not to trust me. Because I was always trying to get her into bed. She didn't want to be gotten into bed. She wanted to make raspberry jam, or peanut-butter fudge, or go shopping for a sofa. Sometimes I'd help her make the jam. Sometimes I'd shop with her for the sofa. And then, afterwards, I'd try to jump her. "Is that what you were thinking of all afternoon?" she'd ask. If the denial wasn't forthcoming and also convincing, I would have spoiled the whole day. Sex was one sort of passion, she thought, love another. And the very last thing she wanted was to have me crawling all over her pretty little body. "I'm tired," she'd say, or, "I just took a shower." Or, "I *was* having such a good time."

I feel odd writing about this, because it's not my story alone. It's also her story, and I'm sure she sees it differently. We never agreed on boo. No, that's not correct. Our astonishment was mutual. I couldn't believe this had happened to me. She couldn't believe this had happened to her.

I'd been unhappy. I often thought my destiny tragic, although I always thought it important. Once married, I was still unhappy, but now I wasn't exceptional, either. I was working at a chain newspaper; I was applying for a job at IBM; I was freeloading in a house with color-coordinated toilets.

The girl wasn't used to being unhappy. She was beautiful, and smart, and she did fit in. She was a cheerleader, a member of something called the key club. She could play the guitar. If she dated a musician, then it often turned out that he saw in her a rare musical talent. If she dated an architect, he appreciated her understanding of symmetry. And most of these people never even touched her. Now she was stuck with this one man who had one thought.

We had a son. A boy I lost in the divorce. It was so bad that I can't clearly remember now how bad it was.

I always had a job. Sometimes my employers loved me, sometimes they only tolerated me, but they never hated me. For hatred I had to go home.

I never slept with anyone else. I never even kissed anyone. Sometimes I think that this is because my father was a bisexual, and one of the ways he disguised his bisexuality was to boast about his heterosexual conquests. And I don't know, but maybe he made them seem like work. Maybe I grew up thinking of adultery as one of the odious responsibilities that fall to the grown man, like weeding the walk, or taking out life insurance.

So it wasn't philandering that ruined our marriage. Philandering might have helped. I don't think she philandered, either. Or if she did, it was a terrible disappointment.

If I were going to extract one simple rule from the wreck of that marriage, it would be to not marry a woman who doesn't like her father. Even, and especially, if she says you're so different from the old man. Someday she'll stop making the distinction, and she'll hate you every bit as well as she has hated him.

Also, you do marry the family. So don't ever join a family you can't bear, or one that can't bear you.

My first wife and her mother were in love with each other. That was the great passion. Her mother had to tolerate me in order to get her daughter back. I don't believe that she ever welcomed me. Or even liked me.

My beloved second wife is in love with her father. And he is in love with her. But when I met him in his own house, he took a knife that he had recently found and as we sat and talked, he broke the knife apart. He destroyed it. I don't know if this was conscious or unconscious, but I saw it then, and I see it now, as a beating of swords into plowshares. This man has never stood between his precious daughter and her husband. Never. Not once.

As for my mother-in-law, she likes me, which is great. But also she laughs. She has a sense of humor. And when I define a sense of humor, I don't just mean the ability to chuckle at a TV game show. I mean the ability to laugh when it hurts. Which is always a blessing.

So I suppose it wasn't just the different bride that made one marriage succeed and another fail. It was the different family.

WHICH MEANS you can't just arm the bride and groom. The entire wedding party has to be locked and loaded. Which is, interestingly enough, the first convincing argument I've heard for the legality of assault rifles.

A lot of money could be put in a pot to be divided among the survivors. The clergyperson counts to three, and everybody opens fire.

We could call it war. God knows it would be cheaper than real war, and in most cases it would be more to the point. A bad marriage is much worse than a bad peace.

SO HOW COME my bad marriage finally blew up? It was because of the bicycle. I began to ride a bicycle to

work. The *Reader's Digest* had a public shower. I'd leave
my suits in my closet at the office. Flying down Roaring
Brook Road one day, at seven-thirty in the morning, I
actually began to yodel with pleasure. I was surprised by
joy. Also my father stopped drinking. And maybe that's
not important. And maybe it's the only thing that's important at all. In any case, I could go home if I wanted.
Either way, my sad little life began to lose its horror.
Now it only looked ridiculous.

Suddenly, she wanted a second child. We had one
wonderful boy, but we weren't good to him. How could
we be? She'd stopped eating. She used to have one meal
a day, a cup of frozen yogurt with Sweet 'n' Low on
three frozen strawberries. No, she wouldn't see a psychiatrist, or even a general practitioner. It was her life,
after all, her body.

Then the *Reader's Digest* sent me to California, to
Esalen. That's right. Nothing in this world makes the
sort of sense you'd expect. She called me there to say
she'd had her IUD removed. I promptly slept with another woman. I had to get out of that house before we
had another child, and I knew that the only way to get
out of the house was to get off the high ground.

I took the red-eye home to New York. She'd put
flannel sheets on the bed. From Garnet Hill. Now she
wanted me to screw her. For the first time in years. I
said, "I slept with somebody else." And she said it was
OK. I thought it wasn't OK, and so I left.

I was ecstatic. I'd given her all the money I had—
not much. I even left her my grandmother's Canton
china, but I didn't mind. I used to tell people I wouldn't
care if she took the fillings out of my teeth.

She got married again quickly. To the man I saw opening the car door. When she got married, an old friend asked if I was hurt. I said I was not hurt. "So some other man is not sleeping with my wife," I said.

I'VE HARDLY SEEN her since. Except at the movie theater. I haven't seen my boy at all. Not for more than ten years. He doesn't want to see me. I write him letters. He doesn't answer. He graduated from Dartmouth last year. I have a friend who was there for the ceremony. She saw him. She said he looked good. So maybe he, too, is happier without me.

Of course I swore I'd never get married again. When I was breaking up with my first wife, I made friends with a man who was breaking up with his. We used to run twenty miles together most every Sunday. And talk. I told him that I would never get married again. Never. "Whatever malfunctioned in that marriage," I'd say, "whoever was in the wrong, it wouldn't have happened if we hadn't been together." And he'd agree.

My friend is Cuban, and laconic. I speak two hundred words for every six he speaks. And if it weren't for me, there would be a lot of painful silence. On the other hand, he speaks beautifully. His six words are worth about 194 of mine. We'd gone for a run one day and were in the locker room at the office, changing. For the millionth time, I was making the speech about how I would never get involved with another woman for as long as I lived.

"I'm sure you're right, Ben," he said. "But, you know, it's all you ever talk about."

In three months I was in love again. I fought it. I

raged around and gave this poor girl much more trouble than she deserved. "I can't do it. I've tried it, and it doesn't work."

I knew that if I ever really fell in love again, the world would wobble on its axis. And so it has. Once again I've lost my footing. Once again, the compass has broken. But this time, the world creaked around the other way. And now we face the sun.

BEDROOM

TAPESTRIES

BY *Tim Parks*

A COUPLE OF YEARS ago I found myself listening to a lecture on the somewhat abstruse theme, "Marriage Bedroom Tapestries in the Works of Shakespeare: *Othello, The Winter's Tale, Cymbeline.*" It's not the kind of thing I would generally move heaven and earth to get to, but I was stuck in a conference center at Lake Como, way out of town, it was raining heavily, there was nothing else to do.

As it turned out, I was spellbound. With extraordinary vivacity, the speaker, a fine-looking woman in her fifties, used slides and video clips to illustrate the profound ambiguities of a series of images woven onto the upholstered bedsteads of the Elizabethan aristocracy. Particularly fascinating was the collision of sacred and profane, the scenes of domestic bliss undermined by evident allusions to more disturbing emotions: serpents and harpies warning rapturous newlyweds of obscure calamities to come.

Then the speaker began to explain how Shakespeare had drawn on this material in his plays, but what she really ended up giving us was a whole history of marriage, from its dynastic origins, when the family was everything and sentiments were relegated to extramarital adventures; to the crisis sparked by the tradition of courtly love when husbands and wives began to leave their partners to follow their lovers; and finally to the novel idea that marriage could be founded on love rather than family. This, the speaker claimed, was the subject of the three plays she had selected for consideration, this the underlying theme of the allegories featured in the bedroom tapestries: the huge gamble of placing love at the heart of marriage, the sad discovery, fearfully embodied in *Othello,* that love is even more fragile than dynasty. All it took was an unexplained handkerchief, a jealous temperament, and, as Shakespeare so timelessly put it, "Farewell the tranquil mind!—farewell content!"

So much for the lecture. Over lunch, chatting with two elderly professors, I couldn't help but praise the energy and passion and relevance of the speaker's analysis of marriage. "A brilliant lecture," I insisted. "No mystery about that," remarked one of the two. His smile was at once sad and wry. "Her husband just left her for a twenty-five-year-old."

Love and dynasty, passion and family. It was around this time that Alistair's story got into full swing. I was his confidant. We played squash together twice a week, then over beers afterwards he told me all about it. We were best friends. As he spoke, he was full of laughter and his face burned with excitement. "You've blown your marriage," I warned him. He laughed out loud and used sports terminology. *Playing away. Scoring in extra time. Next week's game plan.* "The logistics can be so complicated," he chuckled. He even giggled. And you could see what an enormous sense of release he felt in this first affair after eight or nine years or marriage. Alistair was a very sober, a very solid, a very reliable man, but now the great dam of vows and virtue, his young man's conventional vision of life, was crumbling beneath a tidal wave of dionysiac excitement.

We worked together at the university and in the corridor I showed him a passage from a book I was translating: Roberto Calasso's *The Marriage of Cadmus and Harmony:*

> Dionysus is not a useful god who helps weave or knot things together, but a god who loosens and unties. The weavers are his enemies. Yet there comes a moment wheи the weavers will abandon their looms to dash off after him into the mountains. Dionysus is the river we hear flowing by in the distance, an incessant booming from far away; then one day it rises and floods everything, as if the normal above-water state of things, the sober delimitation of our existence, were but a brief parenthesis overwhelmed in an instant.

"You're possessed," I told him. Alistair nodded and laughed. He had been a weaver for so long. He had woven together family-house-career-car. But the following evening, after squash again, he was describing how in that family car his girlfriend (though he always called her his mistress) had pulled up her skirt—they were on the turnpike from Verona to Venice—and started masturbating, then rubbed her scented hand across his face, pushed her fingers in his mouth. Since we live in Italy and have both lived here a long time, he occasionally broke into Italian. *"Evviva le puttanelle!"* he laughed. "Long live the little whores!" He was in love with her. For those of us looking on, those of us still safely married, still living safely within everyday limits, it's hard not to feel a mixture of trepidation and envy on seeing a friend in this state. Clearly it is very exciting when you start destroying everything.

Alistair referred to his wife as "The Queen of Unreason" or "She Who Must Be Obeyed." His wife was still a weaver. They had two young children. In the way that feminism has changed everything and nothing, she was in charge at home, she who felt primarily responsible for the children. Men of course now help in the home, and being a reasonable and generous man, Alistair helped a great deal. More than most. But he was not in charge. Her conscientiousness and maternal anxiety, heightened no doubt by her decision to stay at work despite the kids, must frequently have looked like bossiness to him. Their arguments were entirely trivial: whose turn it was to do this or that. He felt himself the butt of her imperatives, his behavior constantly under observation. It's difficult to make love in these circumstances. Or perhaps it was simply that with everything now achieved it was time for something else to happen. All of us have so much potential that will never be realized within the confines necessary to weave anything together. Job and marriage are our two greatest prisons.

When he asked his wife what was wrong, how could he understand if she didn't tell, she said if only he spared her a moment's attention he would understand without being told. Every intimacy is a potential hell. Alistair referred to sex with his wife as "duty-fucking."

The affair began. Chiara was a young widow, thirty-three, with a ten-year-old girl and an excellent job in education administration that took her to the same conferences Alistair attended. Rather than a decision, it was a question of opportunity coinciding with impulse, or rather with a day when he felt he deserved this escape. Sex was new again. They made love in Rome, Naples, Geneva, Marseilles. They made love in cars, trains, boats. They made love in every possible way. No erotic stone was left unturned. Anal sex, water sports, mutual masturbation, I had to listen to it all. And all the complicated logistics of their encounters, which seemed to be at least half the thrill: advantages and disadvantages of mobile phones, the dangers of credit cards. They adored each other's bodies, inside and out. Alistair was in love with Chiara. She was so intelligent. Her black hair, too. Wasn't she beautiful? Between lovemaking they had such intelligent conversations: philosophy, psychology, politics, their lives. They gave books to each other. They swapped stories. They experienced the delirium of all that information flowing back and forth, your own life retold, another life discovered. There is always something to talk about when one is falling in love. As so often there is not in the long-haul mechanics of marriage.

But how could Alistair leave his children? He loved his children, though his wife was becoming more and more difficult. Every now and then he would interrupt his long descriptions of carefully timed meetings and frantic sex with some self-justifying story of his wife's unreasonableness. Why did she always object to the way he did even the most trivial things, the way he hung a picture, the way he left his toothbrush—get this— turned outward from the toothglass, so it dripped on the floor. Can you imagine! he protested. Not to mention the fact that she never gave him blow jobs. But Alistair admitted that he couldn't be sure anymore whether his arguments with his wife were purely between the two of them, or had to do with his mistress. Perhaps he was deliberately stirring up these petty conflicts in order to justify his eventual departure. Perhaps they weren't arguing about a toothbrush at all. Things were getting mixed-up. Out of nostalgia or guilt or perhaps just in order to see what it felt like, Alistair would try to be romantic with his wife. He would bring flowers. When the children were safely asleep he would persuade her to make love. And immediately he realized he didn't really want to make love to her. He felt no vigor, no zest. He wanted to be with his mistress. "I told her I'd heard the baby coughing." He laughed. But sadly.

Passion, family. Was it time for Alistair to leave home? I thought yes. He said when he and his wife sat together of an evening playing with the children or catching a movie on TV, they were perfectly happy. Not to mention the economic aspects. And perhaps the thing he had with Chiara couldn't be turned into long-term cohabitation. He lived in the frenzy of the choice unmade, the divided mind. Convinced he was trying to come to a decision, he relentlessly applied the kind of logic that was so effective in his research, as if this were a technical problem that could simply be solved. It's the Cartesian legacy that has filled the stores with self-help books: Life's a problem to solve if only you know how. I was equally glib. "You've just got to work out which means most to you," I told him. "Perhaps it's only sex with Chiara." "You must never put the word *only* in front of *sex*," he objected. "Or not the kind we have. It's an absolute." "So, you're only staying at home for the children," I tried. "You should leave." But now he said that you couldn't put the word *only* in front of *children* either. Passion and children were both absolutes. You couldn't weigh them against each other. In the end, Alistair managed to prolong a state of doubt and potential, of anything-can-happen precariousness, for nigh on eighteen months. Later he would appreciate that this had been the happiest time of his life.

But Chiara was cooling now. There were limits to this feverish kind of equilibrium. Finally it was decided that Alistair and his wife would take separate holidays. The months of July and August would be spent apart. "Are you sure you mean it?" I asked him. He had begun to phone me regularly, this time to tell me he had told Chiara he was leaving his wife. "After all, that's not strictly true," I said. "You only decided on separate holidays." He said he thought he meant it. Anyway the point was he felt he had to make something happen. It was an expression that stayed in my mind. An expression that gnawed. Perhaps because it was unusually honest. For thinking back now on the many friends I have who have divorced or separated or left their spouses and got back together, or divorced and married someone else and divorced again and married someone else again, it occurs to me that while most of them talk earnestly of their search for happiness, their dream of the perfect relationship, what really drives them is a thirst for intensity, for some kind of destiny, which so often means disaster. It's the same endearing perversity that found paradise so tedious that one way or another that apple just had to be eaten. Man was never innocent. Marriage was never safe. "I have to make something happen," Alistair said. In this finely managed, career-structured world we've worked so hard to build, with its automatic gates and hissing lawns, its comprehensive insurance policies, divorce remains one of the few catastrophes we can reasonably expect to provoke. It calls to us like a siren, offering a truly spectacular shipwreck. Oh, to do some really serious damage at last!

But Chiara said no. Chiara said she didn't want to live with Alistair. She didn't want to risk the happy routine she had built up with her daughter after her husband's death. She didn't want to risk again. She didn't want to be responsible, she said, for ruining Alistair's marriage. They must stop seeing each other completely.

Alistair collapsed. The gods abandoned him. Intoxication was gone. He couldn't live without it. He couldn't live without joy, he said. He crumpled. His smoking shot up to sixty a day. He drank heavily. His wife was alarmed, became excessively kind. This infuriated him. He could barely speak to her. He could barely speak to the children. He could barely see his children. Unable to sleep, he dozed all day. His work went to pieces. And now he tortured himself that if only he had asked sooner, Chiara would have said yes. He had tried to negotiate, to manage things. His procrastination had destroyed her passion. He should have trusted his instincts. Finally I managed to persuade him to see an analyst.

As I said, we live in Italy. It's a country where people divorce significantly less than in the United States, but perhaps have more affairs. It's a country which perhaps never believed that romance should be the lifeblood of marriage (or not after children arrive), a country where a friend of mine told me that at his wedding his grandmother advised him to try to be faithful for at least the first year. In short, it's a place where people expect a little less of each other and of marriage. Above all they don't expect the privilege of unmixed feelings. Hence it's a country where analysts give different advice.

The analyst told Alistair that only the wildest optimist would divorce in order to remarry, presuming that things would be better next time around. Why should they be? Was there anything intrinsically unsuitable about his wife, anything intrinsically right about his mistress? His problems sprung from his Anglo-Saxon Puritan upbringing, from the fact that he'd never been unfaithful before. This had led him to attach undue importance to the sentimental side of this new relationship in order to justify the betrayal of values—monogamy, integrity—that would not bear examination. He had "mythicized" his relationship with Chiara. What he must do now was take a few mild tranquilizers, settle down, and have another affair at the first opportunity, to which he should be careful to attach no more sentimental importance than an affair was worth. Some, but not much. And keep it brief. Meantime he might remember that he had an ongoing project with his wife. They had been through a lot together. They were old campaigners. Think of the practical side. Think of your professional life. He told Alistair that every family was also a business, or *hacienda* as the Spanish say, a family estate, a place where people share the jobs that have to be done.

Is such advice merely cynical? Or in a very profound way romantic? Old campaigners. Discussing it after Alistair had put in a decidedly lackluster performance on the squash court, I felt it wise to agree with the analyst, at least about the ingenuousness of imagining things would be better next time. And I told him that during the Italian referendum on divorce in 1974 one of the arguments against divorce put forward by some intellectuals was that it would change the nature of affairs. I tried to make him laugh. You'd never know if your mistress wasn't planning to become your second wife.

But visions of such consummate convenience leave little scope for myth and misery. Alistair had been in love with Chiara. He had given his heart. Such clichés do count for something, whatever an analyst says. Trying and failing one evening to have sex with his wife, unable to feel any stimulus at all, Alistair suddenly found himself telling her the truth. He didn't decide to tell her, as indeed he had decided nothing in this whole adventure. Everything had been done, usually after enormous resistance, under an overwhelming sense of compulsion. Perhaps this is the way with anything important. He told her the whole truth and got his catastrophe.

Or so it seemed. The wife was destroyed. He had spared no details. She insisted he leave. He did, discovering as he did so what a large space home and children had played in his life. Most of this he struggled to fill with whiskey and Camel Lights in a lugubriously furnished apartment in a cheaper area of town. Legal proceedings had just begun when Chiara came back to him. At this point there was a brief hiatus since Alistair no longer felt the need to be in touch with me. He was so happy. So I heard later. He had won his dream. The hell with the analyst. The hell with squash. The wife, who I always liked myself, was more than generous with access to the children; Alistair was more than generous with money. All was well. Indeed perfect. It was about three months before I got another call . . .

Perhaps what I'm trying to say about divorce is how tied up it is with our loss, our intelligent loss, of any sense of direction, of any supposed system of values that might be worth more than our own immediate apprehension of whether we are happy or not. We are not ignorant enough to live well, too arrogant to let old conventions decide things for us. Put it another way: For many, and especially for men, I think, who do not bear children and do not breast-feed them, the only thing that is immediately felt to be sacred, the only meaningful intensity, or the last illusion, is passion. D. H. Lawrence puts this very simply in *Women in Love*. Birkin says:

> "The old ideals are dead as nails—nothing there. It seems to me there remains only this perfect union with a woman—sort of ultimate marriage—and there isn't anything else."
> "And you mean if there isn't the woman, there's nothing?" said Gerald.
> "Pretty well that—seeing there's no God."
> "Then we're hard put to it," said Gerald.

This perfect union with a woman. Over beers again, depressed and tranquilized, Alistair was explaining how he thought he'd got that, until the night after lovemaking when Chiara casually asked him if he wanted to know the real reason why she had said no to his initial proposal to live together. It was because she had just started an affair with another man. With Alistair being married and mostly absent it was inevitable. She'd wanted to see how it would work out with this man. Quite well, as it turned out. Though he wasn't at your level in bed. She laughed. Alistair hit her.

Alistair now became obsessed by the fact that there had really been no great love. Quite gratuitously, Chiara had exposed the illusion around which he was rebuilding his life. For now she said that she had had three or four other lovers during their affair. Why should she have put all her eggs in one basket and risk getting hurt, she said. Alistair, who had never hit anybody, hit her again. The analyst explained to him that hitting her was his way of trying to preserve some sort of myth, albeit negative, about the affair, trying to insist on its importance. Disturbingly, Chiara appeared to like being hit. She came back for more, told him more. It took them another year and two trips to the hospital to stop seeing each other. It was always she who came back. Alistair told the whole thing to his wife, who commiserated. They made love. They started seeing each other more often. But without interrupting the divorce proceedings. Alistair began a long series of affairs whose main purpose seemed to be to relive the passion of the earlier affair, whose main purpose, perhaps, was to rediscover the enthusiasm that had led him to marry in the first place.

Marriage and divorce are so tangled up with our sense of mortality. One lives such a short time, yet wishes to do everything. Then to recapture everything. Start again, the springtime says. Unfaithfulness never fails to rejuvenate. But if we start again too often, nothing will be brought to completion. And happiness? That long-term monogamy is unnatural is something every male of the species has felt. Yet where would we be without some repression? The perfect union begins again. Another intimacy beautifully galvanized by the unbridgeable distance between men and women. A radical incomprehension. The children arrive. There are disagreements. The project falters. Our biology has little time for wholesome values and domestic routine now the reproduction is done. The sound of a river in the distance lifts your head from the loom. The sound of rushing water. Time to batten down the windows, sandbag the doors. Old campaigners will take their kids to baseball or take up baseball themselves. Or piano. Or drawing classes. Or martial arts. In a chaos of receding floodwater, Alistair surveys his rearranged landscape. He has the kids alternate weekends, eats regularly with wife and family. Sometimes it's hard to tell whether they're separated or not. The analyst has become a friend, plays squash with Alistair and swaps stories of affairs over beers. His main boast is three in three days at a conference in Palermo. The divorce has come through at last. As divorcés will, both Alistair and his ex-wife assure me, perhaps a little too insistently, that this is the ideal solution.

GETTING THE POINT

BY *Ted Solotaroff*

MOST MARRIAGES do not separate equally.

I've been through three separations, and each time I appeared to have the long end of the stick. My wife was left in the dismembered household with the troubled child or children, while I went forth to my new flat and free time. She had a new and difficult life to put together, while I went on, more or less, with the one I had been leading when I was away at my office or working in my study, which was most of the time. She had to make do on a reduced income, while I had only to provide my share and could moonlight more easily than before. She had to deal with the isolation of the single woman while I had only to pick up the phone to become an available man. Each breakup was a shattering experience, but the evening after I moved out, there I was, forlorn but high and dry, arranging my books the way I wanted them, cooking a favorite dish, an evening of undistracted contemplation of the irrevocable before me. It's as though after a serious car crash, my wife remained inside to extricate herself and the kids from the wreckage, while I opened the only working door and went off to recuperate, promising to send money, phone the kids, and stop by on the weekend to take them off her hands.

Along with typically having easier circumstances to contend with, the husband of a failed marriage is likely to suffer the failure less intensely. Traditionally, the man provides for the family while the woman maintains it, and though these roles are no longer as clear-cut, they haven't been canceled. The woman generally puts more of herself into the marriage and sacrifices more of herself in holding it together. The chances are that the man is the one who has been straying, or if both are unfaithful, he is the one who started it, his biology as well as his buddies prompting him to do so, society winking at his roving moves and saying that's the way the cookie crumbles. So, while the wife still has two feet on the platform, he already has one foot on the train and the breakup places him on his own two feet and on the move, feeling ten years younger—except when the kids visit: Fathering after divorce is a whole other subject that I don't want to go into here.

There is also his work. Most men do better at work than they do at home because they have to be more grown-up there—more temperate, responsible, dedicated, focused, sensible. The blowups and sulks that the man of the house visits upon his wife and kids he spares his colleague and assistant. If he listens carefully when he loses his head, he can usually hear the voice of his own dominant parent that he is parroting. Also his work habits are built on a later, less vulnerable stage of the self than his family ones. Finally, his work is where he still belongs. So for eight or ten or whatever hours a newly separated man puts into it, his job or profession helps him to settle down again, to rejoin the person he was before the crash and to get on with his life.

Getting on with it, putting the problem behind you, is what men are trained to do. You hear one or another of the resolutely forward-looking phrases on almost any given day in the media of sports. A team is blown out by forty points. A popular coach is fired. A key player is injured. The remedy in each case is "I/we have to put it behind us and go on." This is the damage clause of the male code that boys grow up with, the "down-but-not-out" rallying call that gets the testosterone and adrenaline flowing again. It's not just President Clinton who wants to be known as the Comeback Kid. Comebacks are the heroic form of competitiveness, and competitiveness is what masculinity is supposed to be about.

All of which painfully comes back to mind when I think of my behavior in the aftermath of each separation, and all of it adds up to a great big error of good sense and feeling. When a marriage that is meaningful ends, it is not like a lost tennis match or business setback; it is more like the death of someone once loved whom you have been a party to doing in through betrayal, negligence, selfishness, stupidity, or whatever mode or modes of malfeasance and malpractice you committed your share of. What is needed is not to just do something but to sit there with the guilt and grief—to mourn and learn and begin to atone . . .

This would seem to be obvious, if only because the deterioration of a marriage is so rich in experiences of grief and guilt. Genuine marriages don't just end like a game or a job—they succumb. That is, they fall seriously ill and must be attended to and remedied if they are to survive. This crisis ushers in the final stage, usually known as "trying," which emerges from the hollow feeling in the pit of the stomach that follows the rage and hate once one begins to contemplate the abyss that you have just been driven to the brink of. After this sudden empty feeling—the foretaste of the losses of separation—sorrow and guilt spring up to fill the void and to counsel remedies, bringing with them empathy and contrition to ground the "new understanding" that enables the marriage to continue to the next crisis. One of the most reliable symptoms of a failing marriage is that the couple is most compatible when they are discussing their incompatibility and how to repair it, that is, when the feelings of guilt and sorrow and atonement are most on tap.

However, once the separation is in place and the pit opens for the final time, it is much easier—and probably more enabling in the short term—to fill it with anger and blame. These feelings help to get the man out of the house; they help him to grit his teeth and make the arrangements to leave. They also help to clear his decks for action to deal with his new feelings of intense loneliness. There is something almost biological about the loneliness of the recently separated husband. No matter how strained the marriage had become, he badly misses the warm body in the warm bed. No matter how embattled his family life during the breakup, he still feels more often like a home-loving man without a home than the liberated spirit who is about to play the field.

Such was my loneliness that I began dating almost immediately, after the three breakups occurred. And such were my needs and habits of husbanding and domesticity that before a month was over I was head over heels in a new relationship which, when a child came along, turned into a marriage—one that I was still unready for, having married the first time at twenty-two. This happened not once but twice. Live and unlearn. Dr. Johnson said that a second marriage is the triumph of hope over experience, to which I would add that the third is more like the triumph of compulsion over both.

Hence the need to experience fully the guilt and grief—the teaching feelings of a failed marriage. I didn't begin to get the hang of doing so until the third one was breaking up. This time I was the betrayed party (though I had done plenty of betraying myself) and clearly the one being shed. When the abyss came my way again, I drew back in alarm and spent most of the next nine months camped on its edge, looking the other way, doubting the evidence of my senses and intuitions in order to hold what was left of the marriage together. It was an unprecedented experience for me, not only in marriage but in life, because it turned me into a wife.

That's how I felt or, rather, came to understand the feeling. I became the suitor rather than the suited, which is supposed to happen before marriage not after, when, in most marriages, the two roles customarily are reversed. I not only began to cook, but to plan her favorite dishes. When she had an important paper to write, I was right there to look after our son instead of being away at the office until seven-thirty or burrowed into my study. For the past ten years I had been editing a magazine more or less by myself, but now I would find myself on Broadway in the middle of the afternoon making two copies of her M.A. thesis. That summer we visited my brother and after two days he said that he hardly recognized me, so doting and falsely cheerful had I become in trying to refit this sinking marriage.

Of course, it didn't work and by the end I was sufficiently detached by resignation and anger to get through the ordeal of packing up my books, once again, under the eyes of another child. And almost as soon as I'd gotten them put away on their new shelves, I began my recuperation process in the arms of a former girlfriend. I didn't even wait long enough to get lonely this time. Guilt? Grief? Atonement? I'd been acting on them for the past year. Or so I told myself...

The next three months were the romantic/erotic time of my life up to that point. On the third try I finally became the single guy who wasn't secretly looking to get married again. This wasn't entirely my doing but owed a good deal to the fact that my passionate friend was fitting our affair into an active schedule of them. Nonetheless, I was dazzled to discover I was no longer jealous. At age fifty I was finally beginning to get it right. Or, as my friend put it, "You've adapted to the singles scene. I didn't think you would."

Nonetheless, she dropped me. "Too much pressure," she said. I was too busy happily chipping away, extracting the gold from the rock face, to notice that the timber of the mine was creaking. When it gave way, I was at first stunned and then overwhelmed and then devastated.

It was not just this relationship that had given way, but the whole defense, of which it was the center, against the accumulated, unrequited guilts and griefs of all my marital failure. Its abrupt collapse produced a cave-in.

For the next several weeks I limped around emotionally, using my work as a crutch, my four sons as a brace, yoga exercises and meditation as a kind of liniment, Valium as a sedative; the pain of abandonment and remorse never more than a thought away. I had bought a kitten for my fourth son, who stayed with me almost half of each month, whom we called K. I had never been much for pets but *faute de mieux* (unintended), I began relating to this one, who seemed to climb into my relentless sadness and keep me company. Then, one weekend in early March, driven by the miserable prospect of spending it alone in my flat, I took her with me to a house that a friend let me use in Amagansett.

The first day seemed a huge mistake, for as it happened I had been there at one happy time or other with each of my three ex-wives. When I couldn't face those memories and the regret they tipped over any longer, I put K in the car and drove to the beach on what seemed like a bright early spring morning. Another mistake, as I immediately realized when the wind off the shore hit me full blast, penetrating my thin jacket as though I were nude. I walked about a hundred yards; though the wind was at my back, it was still too much even for my masochistic state, and I took shelter on the lee side of a dune. K kept trying to squirm into my lap, probably for warmth, and in my bitter mood I pushed her away and finally picked her up and flung her like a chest pass off into the sand. She picked herself up, stared at me, as though in perplexity, and then settled on her paws, still watching me. Then came the thought, as strong and bitter and chilling as the wind, that what I'd just done to K, I had, sooner or later, one way or another, done to each of the women who had been closest to me.

During the past month I'd wept once or twice, but it was a trickle compared to the storm waves of guilt and grief that rolled over me now, tossing me about in memories and images of abandoning each of my wives in turn until I'd worked my way back to my mother. I'd sorely neglected her in her last years when she'd gamely drifted from one warm climate to another looking for one where she could cope with her severe arthritis. With my mother, as with my wives, there had always been the scrim of circumstances and grievances that had enabled me to look away from the culprit within, but now he rose up, both arrogant and needy, naked of excuses, in one situation after another. When I finished weeping for the women, with undiminished force I began weeping for myself, so alone now, so utterly alone. And then, back on the shuttle line of grief, I began weeping for them again.

When it was over and I was about to get up and move away, I noticed K who was stretched out in the sand, no longer watching me, no longer tuned into my mood, as inscrutable as a sphinx. I felt too drained, too emotionally feeble, even to try to make amends. Instead I began to study her, soon growing bemused by her intactness, her demonstration of creaturely being-in-itself. She was so, I thought, because she had an inner and an outer and was therefore complete. It dawned on me that so did I. I might be missing a great deal of what I thought of as life, but none of it was essential to being alive, of having a functioning inner and outer, which meant that I was already basically complete. Empty but complete.

This was a new way of looking at things—a stripped-down way that appeared to have come out of my first baby steps in understanding yoga. In time I roused myself, made amends with the still imperturbable K, and girded my body for the ordeal of walking back to the car. But after a few steps I was startled to realize that my body was impervious to the freezing wind, that some brand-new heating unit had turned on in my chest and belly and was radiating warmth to my limbs and face. I hadn't been practicing kundalini yoga as such, but it was now practicing me, and I walked up the beach bearing my cylinder of radiant energy all the way to my car.

Well, as Saul Bellow puts it in *Henderson the Rain King,* truth comes in blows. I had had a primary lesson in living alone, in self-sufficiency, which paradoxically turned out to be a necessary requirement for a successful marriage. Unfortunately, Bellow is particularly wise in using the plural, for it took several other blows before I finally got the point once and for all. "You're a killer," the last victim of my new solitary will and my old uxorious ways put it to me. Instead of big divorces, I was now creating little ones, one after another.

Some six months followed in which I saw no one. There's nothing like a lot of Saturday nights alone for your inner and your outer to get to know each other and, no matter how much yoga you do, to begin to get tired of each other. On one such evening, fairly far along in the moratorium, my inner said to my outer, "Look, if you had a date tonight, even one that wasn't that exciting, you'd still arrange something interesting and pleasurable to do—a promising concert or play or movie, a nice restaurant. But me you keep sitting here like a wife who is boring you spitless. Why don't you take me on a date?"

Which I began to do. Some of my dates with myself were more interesting than others which barely emerged from the loneliness they were meant to dissolve, usually because I planned them in a perfunctory way, which produced further lessons in self-regard. At the intermission of a play or concert I would study the other members of the audience, particularly my fellow middle-aged singles to whom I would have paid little attention before, looking now for signs of independence and self-sufficiency, for those who were "lords and owners of their faces." Now and then I would see a woman who was my type by herself and was pleased to find that I no longer had the urge to hit on her. I wasn't looking for anyone anymore to expand my possibilities except myself. "I will study and get ready," as Lincoln put it, "and maybe the change will come." And in time it did.

HOW TO GET DIVORCED

A Practical Guide

BY *Michael Ryan*

1. IF SOMETHING ABOUT YOUR WIFE BOTHERS YOU, SPEAK RIGHT UP!

There's really no good reason why your wife can't be better in every way, if only she would try harder. Scrutinize her aloud on a daily basis. Don't overlook anything. Consolidate the most desirable qualities of every woman you have ever met, seen, or imagined, and measure her against that ideal. Physical flaws are particularly potent. When she orders something fattening in a restaurant, make a face. Then follow it up with a witty sarcasm as soon as the waiter's out of earshot. If there's nothing about her body to criticize—if she's one of those women who spend more on her personal trainer than the gross national product of Uzbekistan—point out other women you find attractive whenever you're in public together. At home, use TV shows and fashion magazines. Pick women with completely different body types. If your wife's tall and slender, go for short ones on the chubby side. If she's blonde, mention in passing that you've always had a thing for redheads.

Character flaws are good, too, although nobody really cares that much about character anymore. Sure, happiness is still important to people, but everybody knows there's no getting it these days without money, fame, power, and beauty—or at least three out of the four. Still, if she's not overly generous or kind, mention it frequently. Maybe she had some sort of childhood religious training that still makes her guilty. Plug into it whenever the opportunity arises. What has she done lately to stamp out world hunger? Has she made a truly sincere effort to save the Amazon rain forest? Think of the issues dear to her heart, then nail her on them.

Another great technique is to praise people you know she doesn't like. Contradict her when she says something negative about them. If she's got a running argument, especially with a member of her family, take the other person's side. Present this in the context of being objective and reasonable and helping her to see the truth.

Money's always a good issue. And it's double-pronged. One prong is how much she makes (warning: Do not use this prong if she makes more than you). Slighting comments about her career prospects, while effective, are rarely as good as slighting comments about her actual salary. "You don't make enough to pay for your gas" is a tried-and-true standard, but, if that's too obviously hyperbolic (or she commutes by train), for "gas" you can substitute "wardrobe" or "the day care" or, best of all, "lunch out." Can you hear the little snap in that sentence? "You don't make enough to pay for lunch out." Practice saying it in front of the mirror with a dismissive sneer that will remind her of her dad.

Let's not forget this is the nineties. We're smack dab in a two-earner-income economy, and by this time your wife knows she should be Having It All, so if you do have kids, don't let it temper your carping. Contrast her cooking and housekeeping to your mother's when you go out to celebrate her promotions. Remember, every mother is terrified that she's a bad mother. The teeniest suggestion can send an otherwise well-adjusted woman into paroxysms of guilt, which can then be manipulated to get something you want.

The other money prong, of course, is how much she spends. This should not be a problem, because no doubt she actually does spend too much. Certainly, hit the big-ticket items with all you've got, including her wardrobe for work. "Three hundred bucks for *that* dress?!" is another one of those old standards that have served mightily since the little woman stopped making her own clothes out of homespun. But don't restrict your criticisms to her expensive personal items. While she's unpacking groceries, having shopped for an hour and a half after ten hours at the office, be sure to point out that at least one of the name-brand products she just bought is selling at the A&P for two-thirds the price.

2. STOP HAVING FUN!

This is tricky, because you and your wife probably wouldn't have gotten married in the first place unless you had been having at least a little fun together. I very much admire my ex-sister-in-law's second husband (she is a psychiatrist and has had six husbands so far): When they got home from their honeymoon, he turned on the TV and sat down in front of it. Brilliantly, during their engagement, he had never watched TV in her presence. Not even a half-hour sitcom. But after they were married, he watched it *all day*—soaps, game shows, congressional committee hearings on prayer in the schools. When after six months of this, she told him she thought they had a problem, he said, "What's wrong?"

Most of us are not blessed with such genius, but don't forget the great tool that is only as far away as your remote control. Buy as many TV sets as you can afford, the bigger the better. If you can afford only one, install it in your bedroom. A forty-incher in a small bedroom can blunt the strongest physical attraction between the most ardent newlyweds.

It goes without saying that, whatever means you employ, you should stop talking to your wife about anything of emotional significance as soon as you are married. If you don't have a TV in the dining room, read a newspaper during your meals at home together. When through careless lack of foresight you find yourself face-to-face with her with no distraction or impediment to intimacy, discuss practical matters only. When she starts to tell you about something that happened at work or a problem a friend of hers is having, ask if she thinks now would be a good time to replace the gutters. A movie together will not be damagingly intimate as long as you disagree with everything she says about it afterwards. Try to draw connections between her opinions about the movie and her poor ethical judgment and pervasive bad taste.

Perhaps you were an active couple before you were married—cycling, swimming, hiking in the mountains in the glorious sunshine, maybe camping together and romantically sleeping under the stars. Join a bowling league instead, preferably five or six bowling leagues. Take up poker or pool. If you have a high-powered job, by all means stay at the office until 10:00 P.M. or later, and arrange extended solo business trips to exotic international cities she has always wanted to visit to conflict with her birthday and your wedding anniversary.

Concerts, of course, are completely off-limits, unless it is a form of music she can't stand. If she loves bel canto opera, take her to see *Cats*. Barry Manilow tickets are often available at a discount at the door on the night of the performance. Front-row seats at a heavy metal concert are virtually guaranteed to be a horrible experience for anyone over the age of thirteen.

But radical self-sacrifice like this is rarely necessary. Just insist on doing what *you* want to do and don't consult her beforehand about plans. When possible, leave her home alone. When she suggests doing something together, whatever it is, make that same face you made when she ordered the fattening dish in the restaurant, and lecture her at length about why her idea is boring and/or too expensive. When it comes to entertainment, as in all things, it's *her* job to make *you* happy.

3. SEX!

This is at the heart of the matter, of course. Absolutely key. I hardly know where to begin, there are so many great things to do. Remember: Even the most self-confident woman has plenty of sexual vulnerabilities. In fact, the more self-confident she seems, the more sexual vulnerabilities she probably has.

As a general rule, request sex crudely and refuse it when it's offered. Never make a sexual overture until your wife actually does have a headache, or is at least dead tired at the end of a day when she has received some shattering news. A really nasty yeast infection can also be very good. Kidney stones: excellent. Almost any biopsy that's gynecological. A bad flu may serve nicely, although after it has peaked some women may surprise you, so be careful on day three or four. We belong to the only species in which the female is in constant estrus, so use your judgment and err on the side of prudence.

In any case, do not ever have sex after you've had a nice evening together. Never allow intercourse to result from tender feeling. You have to be vigilant about this, since sometimes you might be tempted yourself. After all, you're only human. But when you sense yourself being stirred in this direction, maybe in that special candlelit restaurant on that special vacation that you've been saving for together all year, when you see her get that special look in her eyes, ask her sharply, "How come you don't suck me more?"

This does take discipline, but the results are worth it. As for refusing her requests for sex, there are just a whole host of ways to do it. Think of creative ones yourself. It depends upon how she makes her request. A sincere statement like "I'd like to make love to you tonight" can best be parried with a big guffaw. Doubling over and falling off your chair with mirth can be an enhancement if you're an expressive person ordinarily. However, never say or do anything you're personally uncomfortable with. In intimate matters, especially, it's a question of personal style.

The main thing is to blame your refusal to have sex on her. This is a subtle rhetorical trick that takes years to perfect, and you probably should not try it if you're still on your first marriage or your wife is a lawyer or debate coach. But blame is always a valuable tool, even when clumsily employed. "You never want me when I want you" is usually enough to snuff out any feminine fire.

Ideally, you'll rapidly bring your marriage to the point where your wife won't be asking for sex at all. Two tried-and-true techniques can get you there quicker. First, talk frequently and in glowing terms about previous wives and girlfriends. If possible, stay in touch with them and have them write and call. Subtly compare your wife's sexual response to theirs and allude to the remarkable ways they knew intuitively how to stimulate your sexual appetite.

Second, flirt shamelessly with your wife's friends and all her enemies. Pat their butts when saying hello and good-bye. Kiss them on the mouth if they'll let you, and I'm not talking a friendly peck here.

With all the incurable STDs these days, adultery, actual and implied, can do wonders. If you can't work an affair into your busy schedule, do what you can to plant the idea that you'd like to have one. Stare openly at other women when you and your wife are in public together. Initiate frequent talks about how it may not be possible for you to stay committed to the marriage.

4. HOLD GRUDGES AND GO FOR THE JUGULAR!

These two are like the mental and physical aspects of an advanced martial art. You may be naturally more adept at one than the other, but with a little practice you can learn to make them work together and become one with the universal force.

Grudge holding is the mental discipline. It's also a private pleasure in itself. There's nothing more enjoyable than a good grudge nursed to perfection like a fine cigar. People do make mistakes, but that's no reason to forget them. Ever. Lock them into your mind. With concentration and attention, this will gradually become automatic, but at first you may have to write them down, including details of when and where and how your wife wounded you. You might want to buy a small notebook for this purpose or open a file on your computer. If you're not the writing type, use a pocket-size tape recorder, and don't hide the fact from your wife that you're keeping tabs. You need only to record the essentials, such as:

8/8/96: Revealed to the Katzes I snore like a moose, over cappuccino at Starbucks: deep humiliation.

8/13/96: My application for Am Ex Platinum Card denied because her delinquent student loan has appeared on *my* credit record!!!

8/14/96: Did not buy me an ice-cream treat when she went to the grocery store for tampons.

8/14/96: Chicken for dinner again!

Obviously, you deserve better than this. This woman is not nearly good enough for you.

Grudges can, of course, be held against every person you know or have ever known (including the dead), but, as my sample log implies, the daily interaction of marriage offers the richest and most constant opportunities for grudge getting and holding of any of your relationships, with the possible exceptions of those with your elderly parents who can barely go to the bathroom by themselves anymore and (for you writers out there) your publisher.

As part of the mental discipline, spend a few minutes before you go to sleep reviewing all the ways during the day that your wife was not sufficiently mindful of the narcissistic wounds you suffered in childhood. Using just one entry on my sample log for an example, you have told her a thousand times that as a child you were not allowed to have ice cream every time any other kid on your block had it. You know it's not adult to want her to buy an ice-cream treat for you twelve to fifteen times a day, but you do expect her to help while you struggle with this unresolved issue. Her not doing so proves she is not thinking of you continuously. You don't believe you're the most important person in the cosmos, but isn't *she* supposed to? Bring these instances to mind before going to sleep and you will find them being creatively incorporated into your dreams. In this way, your grudges will become part of your unconscious, a kind of body knowledge that will result in increased instinctual power and strength in your marital conflicts.

At this point, you're ready to fully engage in the physical aspect of the martial art. You're ready to go for the jugular! Because of your grudge log, you've got plenty of ammunition whenever you have an argument. Don't hesitate to use it, citing chapter and verse. But it will be much more devastating when tailored to your wife's specific vulnerabilities, which no doubt she has confided to you at moments of deep trust. There has probably never been a marriage in which both partners have not revealed directly or indirectly their most painful weaknesses. Turn these against her. Use her own words, but in a whiny tone of voice. The feelings of betrayal this will cause will be almost impossible to eradicate no matter how much you apologize afterwards. Violation of trust can be accomplished in many different ways, including your basic adulterous act, but your wife will experience your going for her jugular as a true expression of your heart of hearts which she is not likely to forget. If you choose only one of the suggestions among the many in this practical guide, choose this one. It's a total knockout!

5. WHEN IN DOUBT, BE SELFISH!

On those rare occasions when you're not sure how to apply this practical guide, this is your rule: me me and more me. As it says under the entry for "Divorce" in the most recent edition of the *Encyclopedia Americana:* "Marriage is in the process of being defined as a temporary relationship, to be maintained only as long as it helps both partners get what they want out of life." That about says it all.

UNCHAINED MALADY

BY *Herb Boyd*

A FEW WEEKS after my divorce was finalized, I came across an article in the newspaper about a poll conducted among African Americans, asking the recently divorced or separated whether they thought their current status was better or worse than being married. Ordinarily, since I have never been polled, such polls and results seem pointless and irrelevant to me. This one, however, was particularly timely, as if the pollster had seen the letter from my ex-wife's attorney and read the divorce decree that set me free from wedlock.

I don't recall exactly what the findings of the survey were, but I vaguely remember that, unlike most of the black men who responded, I did not lament my unmarried status. In fact, I had been separated so long from my first wife that only badgering from my girlfriend—who had her own plans for a trip down the Aisle of Matrimony—prompted me to investigate the actual condition of my marital status. Somewhere during the many years that my former wife and I were separated I had gathered the impression that our marriage was automatically over, had undergone some emotional statue of limitations, and thereby was null and void since neither of us seemed to care.

There is nothing like a long separation to dull the impact of a divorce, especially when the estranged spouse is just as reluctant to proceed with the legal hassle as you are. There was only one thing that bothered me at the outset: What if she should have children while we are separated? What happens then? For some reason it never dawned on me that she might have had the same concern. As it turned out, we both had children during our separation, which, to some extent, eliminated the possibility of our ever repairing our broken marriage.

Ironically, it was our desire for children that had brought us together in the first place. Or, more accurately, she became pregnant, and gallant Herb acceded to her father's demand that I honor his daughter's request for marriage, lest he might find a way to make it extremely uncomfortable for me to continue to live in the same neighborhood or on the same planet. The look in his eyes was almost as menacing as his gruff voice, and if I had to hear the words "till death do us part," I thought, let them come from a preacher. I was nineteen, with an almost brand-new Mercury coupe and several young ladies dying to ride by my side. All my close male friends told me to forget her; it was her fault she chose to screw at the wrong time of the month. Not one of them said one word about my slipping on a rubber for protection.

After long talks with my mother, I decided to do the

right thing. Ma was right: I was just as responsible as my girlfriend was for what happened. We had a small wedding at my wife's aunt's house and except for several intimate friends, it was a ceremony that brought two families reluctantly together, two families willing to tolerate each other momentarily for the sake of ritual and respectability.

There was no honeymoon. We left the reception, opened our gifts at our new apartment, got sloppy drunk, and shared our first night together in a stupor. We had very little to consummate anyway, given nearly a year of battling a herd of wild hormones, blood-hot testosterone, and at last surrendering in cramped positions in the backseat of my car.

During the next several weeks things moved along uneventfully, and then one day while at work I got an emergency phone call. My wife was hemorrhaging. When I got home, her mother and sister had already rushed her to the hospital. She lost the baby. For several days we were both depressed. For a while we grew closer together than ever. But within a couple of months we faced a new dilemma. Should we continue a marriage that we rushed into? Now was an opportunity to end it. Did we love each other? It was a topic we never discussed, which makes it all the more incredible that we decided to stay together.

Six weeks later she was pregnant again. We felt a little bit better about this conception. This was one we had somewhat planned, an outcome that did not catch us by surprise, so we were relatively elated. With so much attention given to the expectant birth, we were unaware that our tenuous ties were unraveling, that we were drifting farther apart by the night. When I told one of my friends about her pregnancy and our difficulties, he said, "I told you so. Never should have married her in the first place. And you are the stupid one because you had a chance to shuck it all when she miscarried and, sucker, you chose to stay. You've made your bed, so go on home and sleep in it."

Perhaps he didn't say it exactly this way; so many years have gone by since then I can barely envision his face, but I think that was the spirit of his message. Other so-called friends were even more caustic with their advice, reminding me that my wife and I had little or nothing in common but the sack. That she was just an ordinary girl from the projects of Detroit who would probably end up with a houseful of babies and that I was smart, talented, and on my way to great things before I was ambushed. Some of the claptrap was delivered to make me feel both good and superior. By flattering me and putting my wife down, they sought to make me feel better, but it didn't always work. Even so, it did remind me of our differences: the fact that she was from a home where the mother and father were there and I had been raised without a father, a condition I was determined not to extend to another generation.

A month or so after our daughter was born, the proverbial crap hit the fan and we almost came to blows. To this day, I can't remember what it was that put us at each other's throats; much of that intense drama is lost in the shadows of the past. I do recall my anger and that I left before choking the living daylights out of her. I stayed at my mother's house that night and returned the next day to talk things over. Another argument erupted, and I slammed out of the door, called a friend who was having trouble with his marriage, and we met at a bar to plot our getaways.

Neither of us had very good jobs, so we made a pact—in two weeks we planned to get a bus to New York City. There was a terrible storm the day we left and my finger was smashed in a closing car door. That is all I remember about our departure. Johnson and I boarded the bus with a certain amount of apprehension, hoping that things would be better in the Big Apple. Whatever the case, since our marriages were shot, we had nothing to lose.

Thus began a long separation that allowed plenty of time for our nuptial drama to fade, for me to assess the mutual damage, to mull over my failed marriage, and to learn that my situation was not uncommon in an era in which an increasing number of black men were separated from, or in the process of divorcing, their mates. And some of their stories were far more alarming than mine.

Ralph was a devout Christian who spent many hours at his church, volunteering for nearly every outreach project the minister announced. His compulsive attachment to the church angered his wife, and no amount of counseling could close the divide that formed between them. Ralph was devastated by the loss of his wife and children. He saw himself as a family man. Now his most precious possession—his family—was gone.

Another friend, Steve, packed his bags and left his wife because she ceaselessly pressured him to join the church. They had met during the civil rights movement and shared a similar political outlook through the seventies. But things changed after she became a Christian.

Steve continued his involvement in various social and political causes, while his wife placed all worldly cares in the hands of her Lord.

Neither my wife nor I ever belonged to a church, though we were often told that it might help our troubled marriage. Organized religion was not a major factor in our lives, nor in the lives of our parents, which placed us outside the common experience of millions of black people. And given the circumstances of Ralph and Steve, the church may be cited as a corespondent in the rupture of their marriages.

The relationship between the church and divorce has a long history among African Americans. While the possibility of divorce, like the recognition of marriage, was virtually nonexistent in the South during slavery, there is scattered evidence of a few occurrences. Shortly after emancipation, black men and women mainly obtained their divorces through the church rather than availing themselves of white law. (The church and its pastors were also instrumental in discouraging divorces, much like Congress did during World War II when it was illegal to divorce a soldier.) Such recourse is hardly surprising, since black people were excluded from participating in most white institutions. Paradoxically, there are several states that partly trace the origins of their divorce proceedings to interracial affairs.

One of the primary reasons for the introduction of the first "bills of divorcement" in Maryland and Virginia stemmed from the adultery of white women with slave men, or white men with female slaves. As Glenda Riley writes in her informative book, *Divorce: An American Tradition,* such adulterous liaisons figured prominently in persuading legislators to enact divorce proceedings. When Dabney Pettus's wife, Elizabeth, bore a mulatto child a year after they were married in Maryland, he filed for divorce. "An 1803 act of divorce returned Elizabeth to *feme sole* status, that of a single woman who could conduct personal business and hold employment, and declared her child 'illegitimate and incapable of inheriting any part' of Dabney's estate," Riley notes.

These black-white liaisons were not limited to mistresses and their slaves; several masters faced divorce after being charged with consorting with female slaves. In Virginia, a woman accused her husband of infidelity, charging that he was "criminally, unlawfully, and carnally intimate" with a slave woman, who later bore a mulatto child.

Gathering statistics on the history of black divorce is extremely difficult. What is immediately discernible in the literature on the black family is the focus on desertion and separation as the cause for marital breakup. When there are figures and discussion about divorce among black Americans, they usually dwell on the proportionally higher number of divorces by blacks than whites, a fact attributed to marrying too young, lower education, and a higher rate of poverty. Racism and discrimination take their toll on black marriages as well. All of these factors certainly hampered my marriage.

Today it seems to make little difference what your age, educational level, and economic status are. Black men and women are divorcing at a record pace, and this includes a coterie of notables. There is nothing new about this phenomenon, particularly among black celebrities. During my years of separation I was comforted to a small degree by the fact that three of my idols, Richard Wright, Ralph Ellison, and Gordon Parks, had also experienced separation and divorce. If they could overcome their setbacks and thrive as authors, then so could I.

Parks, my chosen mentor, wrote about his lapsed marriage with such emotional gravity that I memorized his lines. "Gene didn't have any illusions about me when we got married," he explains toward the end of his memoir, *To Smile in Autumn*. "She knew I was a hopeless romantic with a sense of adventure, and that I liked to live wide and free." Like Parks, I was a romantic full of wanderlust, and perhaps that was the downfall of my marriage. These words and others helped me to understand my plight as a black man, struggling to be a writer, to be a man capable of caring more fully for my daughter, which I had done to the best of my ability during the years of separation. Valuable lessons were learned, too, from one of my contemporaries, who has written poignantly about the process and pain that ended his marriage.

"I murdered my marriage," writer/activist Kalamu ya Salaam admits. " 'Murdered' because although I felt too weary to continue the relationship, I was not too weary to willfully put a stop to the relationship. . . . Although I had never taken the longevity of my marriage for granted, I never expected the relationship to end."

Unlike Kalamu, I did not kill my marriage, but with my wife, allowed it to expire. As a product of a broken home and surrounded by a host of friends with similar backgrounds, I had very little intimate knowledge of two-parent families with children. Later, during my early

_53_
❏
_by_
HERB
BOYD

twenties I became active in the political movement where an anti-institutional mood prevailed, and along with my disdain for the establishment, the status quo, I am sure there was an unconscious rejection of the institution of marriage, which was a typical attitude shared by many of my comrades.

"Each marriage and subsequent divorce is different," said Lester, a longtime associate from the turbulent sixties, "and I know that sounds kind of trite. First of all, I didn't go through the traditional marriage. Like many of our friends in the movement, we didn't need any Western rituals or ceremony to validate our commitment. We pledged ourselves to each other, and later while I was serving a ten-year prison sentence for political activism, she unpledged it."

Lester and his lady met when they both were retreating from organized religion. She professed an emerging agnosticism and Lester was an avowed atheist. She had promised to stand by him during his prison term but was unable to fulfill the vow, subsequently becoming a Muslim and starting a family without him.

Though Lester avoided a traditional marriage, he at least expressed an interest in coupling. This practice has diminished considerably among black Americans. With each year since the 1930s, there has been a trend of fewer blacks entering the conjugal state, and more of them abandoning it. "In 1930," sociologist Robert Staples asserts, "husband-wife families represented 80 percent of all black households but fewer than 40 percent in 1982.... Recent trends indicate an increase in marriage among whites and a decline among blacks." Staples traces this development to the fact that marriage among Euro-Americans has been primarily rooted in property relations while colonized blacks have been largely stripped of their ties to the land.

Economics is paramount to this issue. The lower their incomes, the more likely blacks will fail in matrimony. This, in part, explains why blacks of median income have the lowest divorce rate. Young married black couples with decent jobs, who combine their salaries and cooperate in paying the bills, create a bonding which makes it possible for them to avoid many of the arguments about money that endanger a relationship. The combined income also allows them to participate more widely in the larger society, to take advantage of some middle-class comforts. Even so, Staples concludes that high-status black males often view women as property and impose rigid rules of sexual fidelity on their wives while themselves participating in a number of extramarital affairs.

During our long separation before divorce, my estranged wife and I obviously had extramarital affairs; in fact, both of us for a while had common-law spouses. I never thought twice about this living arrangement being without legal sanction; it was of no great consequence since I had several friends who had common-law wives and were quite happy with their lives. For us there was nothing wrong with common-law marriage; we did not view it as socially deviant behavior, no matter how it was seen by the larger society. In fact, it was recognized in some states and no length of time was specified to make the cohabitation legal. "The white man destroyed our families, broke them up to suit their own material ends and devious purposes, so who cares what they say about how we choose to restructure ourselves," one friend re-monstrated. He and others had similar opinions about so-called illegitimate births. To them, there was no such thing as an illegitimate child.

These were my feelings, too, about the three children I had out of wedlock and the two children my former wife had while we were apart. I claimed hers as my own, supported them, and it was not until they were teenagers and suspected I was not their biological father did I reveal the truth. It did not hamper our relationship, and I am still the only father they have ever known.

But despite all the history, statistics, common-law arrangements, and numerous girlfriends, divorce was still something that lurked in the back of my mind. So long as my marital status had little bearing on anything, I was content to let it be—a kind of "If it ain't broke, don't fix it" attitude. There came a time when I got word that my wife was seriously contemplating remarrying, but nothing ever came of it, and she remains single, though an attentive grandmother to our daughter's two children. Meanwhile, I drifted from one affair to another, and sometimes even used the fact that I was married to curtail any intentions of matrimony by a current girlfriend. All this was fine until I fell in love with a strong-willed woman who insisted I get my act together, clear up my messy marital situation, and prepare for a traditional "with papers" betrothal.

I used a ton of excuses to avoid getting legal, and more than one time thought about putting my foot down or getting my hat. Neither tactic made me happy, and before another was hatched, I heard from my former-wife-to-be and was told she had begun divorce proceedings. Just for a moment, I thought my girlfriend had gotten in touch with her and prompted the move.

In any event, things went smoothly; the divorce was obtained inexpensively and as matter-of-factly as our marriage nearly forty years before. There certainly were no bitter recriminations, none of that rumored low-intensity gender warfare which often accompanies such legal settlements, the kind of mud-slinging acrimony that would make us candidates for one of those talk shows where guests disclose secrets and tell it all to a national audience, although I have yet to see a show where divorce or post-divorce matters was the topic.

Not too long after acquiring my legal freedom, I got hitched again. And were the pollster to inquire how I feel nowadays, I would be glad to submit that the best cure for divorce is marriage, especially a happy one with unrelieved domestic tranquility.

COURTSHIP MODE

BY *Stephen Dobyns*

I AM SITTING by myself at an outside table of a restaurant called El Club on La Avenida El Bosque in Prov-
idencia, an upper-middle-class section of Santiago, Chile.
Around me are several dozen tables of men and women
between the ages of twenty and forty. All are exquisitely
dressed. Few are eating; most have drinks. They seem
charming, intelligent, the sort of people one can imagine
among one's friends. Though there are some couples,
most are in small groups, laughing and chatting, seem-
ingly engrossed with one another. This is an illusion.
Their attention is focused not on their friends but on
their surroundings. They look at the men and women at
other tables while trying to appear disinterested. Quite a
trick.

Next to El Club is a restaurant called the Hereford.
Across the street is Coco Loco and an Au Bon Pan.

Along this section of El Bosque there are eight restaurants with outdoor tables filled by attractive men and women who are intensely, though secretly, concentrated on the comings and goings around them. Waiters in short black jackets carrying silver trays wind among the tables. There is the sound of laughter and phrases of quickly articulated Spanish. It is seven-thirty on a Friday evening in summer and the setting sun turns the smog a beautiful shade of reddish gold.

A spotless red and chrome Harley-Davidson purrs up to the curb. A young man dismounts. His red leather jacket and red leather pants fit so perfectly that they seem painted onto his body. As he removes his red helmet, gold chains twinkle from his neck and wrists. He pauses to tousle his black curly hair, then walks slowly between the tables, his lizard-skin boots clicking on the concrete. Now a black BMW convertible pulls to the curb and two young women get out: short skirts, bare midriffs, skin the golden color only achieved through weeks of solar concentration. They, too, pause to fluff their hair before passing between the tables on their delicate shoes. More people arrive: a steady stream of the beautiful and aesthetically packaged. Their eyes seem to drift over the crowd. They move to tables of friends or find an empty table for themselves. They sip colorful fruit drinks, imported beers, pisco sours. They seem to take no interest in their surroundings, yet they do; they are as sensitive to what is going on around them as a hawk is attentive to a field where rabbits come and go.

This is courtship mode. We are seeing people at their apparent best.

The several hundred men and women who I can

59

❏

by

STEPHEN
DOBYNS

observe from my table are without imperfections. Not only are their exteriors without blemish, but their every breath and gesture is designed to show that their interiors combine the saint, the sophisticate, and the star. Certainly, different tastes are catered to. Not every woman will be attracted to a man in tailored red leather, the very apotheosis of Marlon Brando in *The Wild One*. To set against the ladies with the bare midriffs from the BMW is a startlingly beautiful blond at a table by herself reading a novel by Anne Rice. Some chew gum, some suck mints, some smoke. Some carry briefcases, some carry tennis rackets.

Even though the men and women at El Club have to a degree commodified themselves, it would be wrong to compare this to a marketplace. The fantasies that lie behind these presentations are for the most part noncommercial. Even the young women who hope to marry doctors, hope to marry with love. The man who seeks his own personal Marilyn Monroe yearns for a Marilyn who will understand him.

But who are these people at four A.M. when a passing siren startles them from sleep? They are not sure. As a result, they study the American and European magazines, or the Chilean equivalent, for role models. One can almost tell what movies they have been watching. Some styles are slower to arrive down here than others. For instance, the designer stubble that was lately so popular among men north of the equator has only begun to be adopted here. But no matter the style, the point is to present a facade free from imperfections. This is more than a matter of ugliness or beauty, because many types of beauty are represented. It is about how one embraces life and an aesthetic ideal. It means no imperfections to the marrow of one's bones.

In courtship mode one is promising happiness forever after. One is promising eternal equilibrium, unfading looks, constant devotion, even temper. Here are the perfect fathers and mothers of tomorrow. None of these men and women would ever scream at, physically abuse, or cheat on a spouse. None would ever beat or sexually molest a child. None would be selfish or lazy or terrified. None would crawl drunkenly toward the toilet, hoping to reach the bowl before they vomit. None would become so jagged on cocaine that every other aspect of their life would be tossed on the trash heap. None would hurt someone because it is fun to hurt someone. None would abuse, insult, despise, mock, cheat, persecute, be cruel or indifferent to someone whom they have sworn to honor, love, and cherish. All that comes after.

WHEN I WAS thirty-one, I fell into a correspondence with a woman who was twenty-two. I had published something that she liked and she wrote to me about it. I was charmed by her wit and intelligence and I wrote back. For over a year we exchanged letters without laying eyes on one another. She was a graduate student in poetry and I had just published my first book of poems. Her letters had a brilliance, a life, a humor, an energy, an elegance that led me to look forward to them and to respond eagerly with my own. And my letters, too, showed wit, intelligence, life, etc. After all, I was a writer. Showing off in letters was something I was good at. Did I tell this woman that I drank too much, was prone to lose my temper, was moody, smoked three packs a day, could be an intellectual bully, and liked to have my own way in absolutely everything? No, of course not—I was in courtship mode.

Besides, these defects were things I hoped to put behind me. I didn't like being moody; I didn't understand that I always wanted my own way. As for my temper, I hadn't lost it for a while. Maybe these defects would disappear on their own, wither away like the stub of an umbilical cord. Maybe they were already gone. In any case, when one falls in love, one seems defectless.

Everything was future. Life was so new and fantastic that I could never imagine being unhappy again. I felt like Adam naming the plants and animals. I felt free of faults and flaws. And in our letters we had fabulous conversations. She sent me her poems and I thought they were marvelous. We hinted at meeting and at what we might look like, until finally I could stand it no more and drove five hundred miles to visit her. And even the meeting was wonderful. I thought she was beautiful, sensitive, and intelligent, and she thought similar flattering things about me. Courtship mode: Both of us projected personalities free from imperfections.

There followed a certain progression. A month later after my visit, the woman visited me. A month later she moved in with me. We were together for three and a half years, then she moved out. I am not sure where the love went during that time. In some ways, it never left; rather, it retreated behind a personal defense system, so elaborate that it might as well have been nonexistent. Except that even after we were separated, the love would come out in fits and starts when we saw one another. "Blindingly undiminished, just as though/ By acting differently we could have kept it so," as Philip Larkin wrote. And that was the most depressing aspect of the business, the love hadn't disappeared, it had gone into hiding. It had been pushed aside by all this other stuff: the drinking, the moodiness, the temper, the selfishness. And perhaps she had faults as well, I don't know. I was too busy with my own faults to pay much attention to hers.

Where does this sense of the ideal come from? A friend of mine recently visited Disney World and what impressed her most was the absolute absence of irony. The same can be said of the romantic ideal. Did I take my idea of love from a hodgepodge of *Casablanca, Gone with the Wind* and a slew of Cary Grant movies? After thirty years of looking at the world—though imperfectly—did I really believe in happiness ever after? But even in college I wondered how it was that the young women in Dickens' novels were so attractive while the older ones tended to be shrewish and awful. When had the change occurred? This sense of love, this sense of the true and the beautiful that exists in courtship mode exists without irony or deficiency. It is as if one had been changed from a caterpillar to a butterfly. No, not a butterfly, an eagle. Not an eagle, an angel. The perfection promised by ten thousand romantic novels, movies, and magazines has been at last attained. Everything was golden up ahead. And this woman and I—we had several perfect months before the problems started to arise. And for at least three years after that it remained good, but the problems accumulated like stones on the other side of a balance and the dark periods grew.

There was an awful fatalism to this that led me to watch the impending destruction of the relationship as I might watch an approaching lava flow. In retrospect, I see I hardly did anything to change myself. I grew increasingly defensive and prepared for any attack. We didn't see a counselor; we simply drifted. In the back of my mind was the sense that it was bound to go wrong, that everything eventually went wrong. The clutter of another person's life intermixed with the clutter of my life created problems that seemed impossible to overcome. At one moment I was pledging eternal love and in the next I was screaming that the top had been left off the toothpaste tube. And these other troubles—books rejected, job opportunities missed, even small daily frustrations—became mixed with the whole until the person I loved, the person who had been the single bright spot in all of creation, simply became the person to take my failures out on. Until it all fell apart. How could it not? Whose baggage, whose mistakes—who cares now?

But in putting that relationship behind me, I don't think I accepted much responsibility. Nor did I blame the woman. If life had been perfect, then the relationship would have remained perfect. Or maybe the love had been flawed from the start. Maybe every love relationship was bound to fail. Or maybe I was only able to do well in the mode following courtship mode. Call it infatuation mode: the dessert one eats before reaching the meal. In any case, I never seriously looked into myself and asked what I could change. If I made mistakes, then I had been fated to make mistakes, which is almost like not making mistakes at all. Fate absolves one of personal responsibility.

Two years later I married a woman much like the

other woman I had been in love with and had lived with for so long. Their looks and personalities were not similar, but my first wife was also a graduate student in poetry and she was about a dozen years younger than me. The marriage lasted three years. We had a son we continue to adore, who keeps us in communication. But the relationship followed a progression similar to the earlier relationship: courtship mode, infatuation mode, life. Is *life* what it is? Is that what we call it when our failings and fallibilities rise to the surface? I once read that Cardinal Richelieu only liked kittens; when they reached adolescence, he gave them away. And I ask myself what it was that kept me from reaching the adolescence—not even the adulthood—of any relationship.

Two years after I was divorced, I married my second wife, who I had actually met before my first wife—but that is another story. We have now been married for twelve years. We have had bad places but we have gotten past them. I tend to thank my wife for this. I am the sort of person who, when the sun sets at night, has no faith that it is going to reappear in the morning until I set eyes on it. But she worked to keep the marriage going and taught me to work on it, too, though I am not sure what I have learned. Patience, perhaps. The ability to put aside my own way, my own desires, my own moods for someone else's. Also, I have the continuing sense that this is it. There is no one else I want to love. And after twelve years we have grown into each other to such a degree that without her I am less than a whole. I'm a fragment.

Set against the marriage is courtship mode, infatuation mode, the joys of kittenhood, the fear of decreasing options. Recently, walking through downtown Buenos Aires at night, I thought that as I grew older the women who returned my glance came out on the street later and later. But what attracts me is not women, the simple desire for other women, it is the idea of options, the desire for unlimited choices. To choose to remain with one woman is to accept the limited world of old age. Though I dispute this, at times I whisper it in my own ear.

It is part of the romantic ideal that the promise of a beautiful woman is the promise of eternal perfection. No defects of character, no decreasing desire, no bad times. Consequently when problems arise, it only suggests that perfection still lies ahead with someone else. One doesn't work to fix anything, one moves on. Part of me thinks this is an aspect of human nature. Another part thinks it is a result of advertising, films, media, and popular culture which all seem to be conspiring to make us believe in an eternal present. And part may be in the allure of other: the self-deception that life, a richer life, is always elsewhere.

At El Club, I sip a fresh raspberry juice. I find myself astonished by the illusion which I see around me of eternal beauty, of an unending present, of relationships that never suffer a decline. That is the promise that seems offered here. Am I the only one foolish enough to believe it? Is no one around me thinking past a possible one-night stand? There is the sense that each of these people feels that his or her life will be made complete by the acquisition of a perfect other, and so they, too, have fashioned themselves into images of perfection from pop culture prototypes.

Let's say some of these couples come together, just

as I did with different women. What happens when imperfections arise, when infatuation mode is left for life itself? Surely the fact that almost half the marriages in the United States and Chile end in divorce suggests something is askew. When I passed beyond infatuation mode into the uneasy realities of life, I did little to save the situation. When problems arose, I junked the relationship and got another. This is the throwaway society. Shirt rips, trash it. Car turns out to be a lemon, sell it. Wife develops problems, find another. There are hundreds of reasons why this is wrong. Life isn't a matter of constant expansion, constant increase. The belief in perfection is an impossible ideal. A refusal to change or admit mistakes is a refusal to move past childhood. Always to blame the other is a denial of one's responsibility. Constantly to shed the imperfect is an attempt to remain in an eternal present, a sort of mall time or casino time: no night, no day, no life passing.

The illusion of perfection is a rejection of mortality. We are toy automobiles chugging along the arcs of our lives: Rust develops, engine coughs begin to occur. Sometimes I feel that my adolescence extended into my midforties, followed by a period of disappointment from which I am just now crawling free. I don't want to suggest that I have the answer; possibly my present marriage will end next week. Still, I have learned that I have to work on my marriage each day and I have to change myself. But it is more than that. I have grown tired of kittenhood. And I feel that the intimacy I have with my wife after twelve years of marriage and nearly twenty years of knowing her is more exciting and sustaining than what I can find in infatuation mode.

Possibly I could have attained this same state with

the other women with whom I was involved for long periods of time, but I didn't have the patience, the maturity, or the wisdom. Mistakes and difficulties began to accumulate so I decided it was time to bail out. Instead of trying to change myself, I changed the situation. I fled not only from the women but myself. Now I don't want to do that; or rather, my desire to stay with one particular woman makes me willing to do whatever I can to permit the marriage to continue, no matter what.

SITTING IN El Club, I love looking at the people around me and imagining their lives. They are pretty. Watching them is like watching butterflies flutter within a garden. Not that I can be completely disinterested in my observations. If one of these beautiful women came up to my table and said, "I want to have sex with you," or the Spanish equivalent, it would be hard to keep my pulse from going crazy. But basically the idea is exhausting and I don't want such adventures. However fantastic it might be, it would be less than what I have. Its sweet whisper is only the allure of the other, the idea that nicer things are happening in farther rooms.

And these people: Statistically they are in for rocky times. Thousands of heartbreaks and disappointments lie ahead in their pursuit of the eternal present and the forever undiminished. Far wiser to embrace human totality, farts and perfumes intermixed. "Love me dirty," said Chekhov, "anyone will love me clean." Far wiser to embrace the single constant of human life which is change itself. Constant motion, constant permutation, constant transition, then death.

I say this, but I don't have it quite clear yet. I come

to El Club partially to remind myself. I come for the view, for all the beautiful people. I come to feel grateful that I am not a part of it. I come to remind myself of what I have. Courtship mode is exhausting. I am glad to scratch and sweat and be human. And I need to repeat this to myself. If someday I am to believe it completely, then I need to say it again and again.

69

❏

by
STEPHEN
DOBYNS

THE

EX-FILES

BY *Michael Ventura*

ABOUT TWO YEARS into my marriage I walked into the living room of our small apartment and saw my wife sitting on the couch. She looked at me. There was nothing at all dramatic about her expression, and yet it was like nothing I had ever seen upon her face. I remember it as a face stripped raw—the face of her face, it seemed. I'm not certain anymore that my perception was true, but that is how it appeared to me at the time. She seemed suddenly a stranger. Eerily so, because everything else about this stranger was more than familiar, was a part of me, except her expression—and, in particular, her eyes.

As soon as we spoke the stranger disappeared and the woman I thought I knew came back into focus. I don't remember what we said then, but I remember what I did next. I went into my writing room and closed the door behind me. (It was the biggest room in that four-room apartment, which tells you much of what you need to know about the marriage.) I sat down, disoriented, baffled, wondering how in more than two years of intimacy I had never seen that face. And I said aloud to myself: "Who *is* she?"

The question frightened me. That's putting it mildly. I didn't think to ask whether the difference was possibly in *me* that day. (Which tells you something else you need to know about the marriage—my side of it, anyway.) I didn't even ask myself why I was frightened. Not that "Who is she?" was such a bad question. I should have asked it long before. But my fear overwhelmed that crucial question, and drove me far from the possibility of any answers. In fact, I was *so* frightened that I instantly forgot the real question and made a lot of "meaning" out of the moment.

That's what I do for a living. I'm a writer, I affix meanings to moments—often too quickly, by reflex. One makes a lot of excuses for such things, but the truth is: There are corruptions inherent in every profession, and to leap (or retreat) into "meaning" is one of the corruptions of mine. For it is no small crime to cram a moment with meaning as a substitute for *experiencing* that moment. I didn't know this then. I didn't know that most writing is just an attempt to control the unpredictable reverberations of an experience—to put a stamp on it, own it in some way, and then (not incidentally) sell it.

So I would make a kind of legend of any event, replete with footnotes—psychological, mythological, sociological, and most of them, in retrospect, more or less illogical. Oh, they sounded impressive in conversation, my little meanings, and they looked good in print. But they didn't help much in the long run, and that *is* the only test, isn't it? Because while I could speak and write some good words, I didn't know how to *do* the words. Which is to say, I didn't know myself. I was afraid to know myself. And it is not possible to know another person when you are afraid to know yourself. So this moment, when I realized that I did not know my wife, was especially terrifying because something in me sensed that I could only know her by first facing myself. I wasn't ready for that. My terror kept me from knowing both of us.

No marriage can survive that much unknowing.

I realize now that my fear was a form of respect—it measured the depth of my real respect for her, as opposed to my imagined respect. "Any human touch can change you," James Baldwin once wrote. My fear gauged both her capacity to change me, and my terror of that possibility. When you live in a profound and almost willed ignorance about yourself, change is far more frightening than it would be if you stood on firmer ground. For not to know yourself is not to know where your real boundaries are, so you remain in constant fear of losing or giving away your soul.

I thought I'd married in order to change, and to commit to love and to being loved, and I had. But secretly, I'd also married to find a haven, find some safety. I had not yet accepted that safety is not a human possibility. The second impulse (safety) undercut the first (love)—because, as with most people, *safety* for me meant some illusion of control. I sought to control my household, as though that would protect me from something. And what I couldn't control, I ignored, or ran from, or tried to stamp down. In other words, I tried to control everything but myself, while running from myself at the same time.

I was thirty-seven when I married, and it's too late to be embarrassed at the fact that I hadn't yet grown up. If I'd been behaving like a grown-up, I might have realized that when I saw that face—when, for a moment, I let myself realize that I did not yet know my wife—*that* is when the marriage might have had a chance truly to begin. For not until the illusions of knowing are stripped away does anything really begin. A braver, more mature, more intelligent man might have committed then and there to the real marriage, instead of the marriage we'd been trying to invent. As it was, my behavior went from difficult to impossible. She was willing to endure that behavior longer than I. She was willing to do the work that may or may not have kept us married. But I had become impossible to myself, I couldn't bear myself any longer, couldn't bear who I'd become in that marriage, and who I wasn't. So, in as destructive a way as I could manage, I ended it. I ran as fast and as irreversibly as my compulsions and neuroses could carry me.

I was suicidal, I was sexually obsessed with other women, I drank too much (way too much), I couldn't really hear what other people said to me, I went into debt, I sold out my talent. Not only the marriage but some cherished friendships got caught in the crossfire that year. My first novel got bad reviews, and just around then my mother died—you know how it is with favorite sons and their mothers.

I had some luck though, and found some new love. It didn't last long, but in a terrible year it did save my life. Love can do that sometimes, remember? (My wife's love might have saved me, too, but I was too far gone to let it.) The young woman I became involved with made me think that there might still be something beautiful about me, and so perhaps I didn't need to die, perhaps my damaged beauty should be given another chance. Others were trying to tell me this, but I couldn't believe them. I believed her.

I also eventually figured out that a settled life is not something I do well, or *want enough* to do well. In trying to be married, at least in the way my wife and I had gone about it, I was violating my nature. The violation may have been an honest mistake, but that doesn't help matters any. A man on the run from himself invites such mistakes, and, as often as not, seduces other people into helping pay for them.

To accept that a settled life is not your lot is to accept that every day you will be thrown entirely upon your own resources. But any life, settled or not, needs a sense of dignity to be lived well. That is most of what growing up means, to attend to one's life with dignity, endure the lacks, relish the pleasures, and not spread the pain around too much.

I learned that much, I guess. But the truth is that I'm not particularly thrilled about how I learned it, and I'm really not thrilled about how my education was paid for in pain by two of the people I've loved most in this world, my ex-wife and my stepson.

You might ask, "How could you have loved her if you say you didn't know her?" I don't know the answer to that question, but I know I loved her. I doubt a day goes by that I don't think in some way of my ex or my son, and I doubt a day ever will. That hurts, but it proves something: I loved them then, and I love them still.

I haven't seen my ex in several years. We communicate now and again, and it's friendly enough. Except while the breakup was going on, we've never talked to each other about the marriage or the divorce, and we both have our reasons. Maybe she's too proud to be my friend, and I respect pride. Maybe I'm too vulnerable to be hers, and I've learned to respect my vulnerability. Or maybe she's too vulnerable and I'm too proud. Or maybe we'll be friends one day, who knows? Or maybe we'll never see each other again. I don't expect to know any of these things with certainty.

But I do know that I broke a vow—a wedding vow that I had given with all my heart, or at least with the part of my heart that I knew about. It is a kind of death to break a vow, and you live afterwards knowing that you are the kind of person capable of breaking the most solemn promise you ever made. You can't help trusting yourself less after something like that. If you're half-honest, you at least learn to be a lot more careful about what you tell people.

Especially when you talk about love. I have come to think that the word *love* is a reckless, sweet invention— even when it's not used as a synonym for *need*. Now I try to reserve my recklessness for my writing and my vices. At the age of fifty, I haven't given up on love, no matter how frayed I sound; but I think of it as word in a foreign language, the pronunciation and meaning of which I only partly understand.

DON'T MISTAKE all this for guilt. I don't trust guilt, at least not mine. It's usually a way to make other people feel sorry for you—or to con them into thinking you're better than you are, for look at how much you've suffered! Don't mistake this for grief, either. Grief, in our glib nineties jabber, is usually just another con, a socially acceptable form of guilt. And for mercy's sake, let's not talk about "growth." If it's growth to leave some lies behind, then I've grown. (Though it may be that I'm just more tired.)

Let's not pretend that divorce is about anything but failure. You tried something important. Whether it was reckless or silly or inspired (or all of the above), it was still important. You wanted something, or thought you did, and you went all out to get it. You broke your heart, or somebody broke it for you, or both. You behaved stupidly or badly or well—or all of the above, by turns. You didn't know what you needed to know until it was too late—and you felt lucky to know it even then.

You can blame yourself or somebody else or everybody. You can blame gender conditioning or your parents or your religion or your education or your lack of it. You can blame your work or your inability to find work that is truly yours. You can blame your desires. You can blame your youth or your age. You can become friends with your ex or not. You can get vicious about the money and property, or not. You can act with dignity or compound your foolishness, or both. You can tell yourself, your friends, and your therapist great tales, and come to marvelous conclusions. But you tried something important and you failed. You hurt others, you got hurt, and you failed.

Of course, failure is not confined to divorce. Many a marriage is a walking failure—people joined in a pact not to know themselves or one another, who try to pull that not-knowing around themselves like a shield against the world. Nevertheless, to be divorced is to *know* you tried something and failed. Your walk changes, your talk changes, your very reflexes change. The way you make love changes. The kind of people you love changes.

Yes, life *is* change, and you would have changed anyway, for better and worse. Some people say all things happen for the best, but no one can prove that. People talk about karma, about "inner children," about all kinds of things, but no one can prove any of it. What I know is that I tried something, and that it was important to me, and that—on its own terms, terms I thought were crucial at the time, no matter how much I've "grown" since—I failed.

Divorce means carrying that around. It may weigh you down or you may have learned to balance it, but you carry it. It may be something you can share or something you can't, but you carry it. You can achieve the dignity of not making the same mistake again, or you can relentlessly repeat your mistake, but either way you carry it. Most things you say about it won't make much difference to anyone else (especially your ex). Others may or may not be moved or enlightened or entertained by what you say, but they'll make their own mistakes anyway—which they'll carry. Life is about carrying stuff until you drop. (Drop dead, I mean; you never drop the stuff.) That's what the lines in your face are about. That's what that hesitation before you say the word *love* is about.

Beyond all that, the history of marriage as an

institution is larger than any of our personal histories, and we carry *that* too. For tens of thousands of years most people lived in tribes, in villages, and on farms, and marriage was essential to survival. It depended so little on romance that most marriages were arranged. The arrangers didn't care who was in love with whom, they cared about what match was best for the survival of the clan. Married people needed to work together; they also needed to work with everyone in the larger social unit. (You need a lot of taboos to keep something like that going.) Necessity determined relationships. It may not have been fun, or fair, or satisfying; but it worked, on its own terms if not on ours, or we wouldn't be here.

Even sixty years ago in America, many of the old ways still held. But advances in technology, during and after World War II, enabled individuals to survive on their own. Marriage was no longer a matter of necessity, so the morality supporting marriage broke down. (Can we call it *morality*, then, if it was really an adaptation to the demands of survival?) For the next half century marriage depended almost solely on a man and a woman's feelings for one another. Feelings being volatile, marriage became volatile. Now that economics has changed again, and two people must work to earn what one earned in my youth, the divorce rate has stabilized. Some statistics indicate it's declining. Necessity, again. But for the more or less affluent, nothing has changed yet. Marriage is still a choice, not a necessity—still depends on feelings, not survival. "Getting in touch with your feelings," as our modern phrase goes, may be important, but feelings are clearly not enough to hold half our marriages together. (The divorce rate peaked in the 1980s at about 50 percent.)

What we're left with is the need to have and rear children without any dependable format for doing so and the need for companionship and community in a technological environment that creates more and more fragmentation. What are we supposed to do with that? Nobody knows. Every day is an experiment now. Welcome to the laboratory of the twenty-first century. We still get married, bless our hearts, and with the best intentions. But it's a form created for a world that's gone, and nothing can change that. Our floundering, our bafflement, and our failure should come as no surprise.

It's good to have some historical perspective on these things. Still, after the divorce, the analysis, the perspective, what we *feel* is failure—failure that our love was not strong or wise or deep enough, or failure at falling for such a bitch or bastard in the first place, but failure either way. It's a lot to carry.

IN MY CUPBOARD are two coffee cups my wife and I drank from. In my closet there's a leather jacket she bought me, and a box containing a game the boy and I used to play. In my bathroom, hanging from a hook, is a many-colored terry-cloth robe she gave me. I've moved several times since the marriage, but I've never thrown this stuff out. Maybe it's nostalgia, or maybe I'm punishing myself, or maybe I sometimes like to think of that year or two when just to see her walk across a room delighted me, and when nothing made either of us so happy as our boy's laughter.

I know I'm not going to throw out the robe or the cups or the game, the way I know I'll never stop carrying what I carry about us. It all feels lighter now, but there are times when it comes back full force. When it does, I take a drink or take a walk or sit with a cigarette and look out my window and lose track of time.

One moment still crystallizes all the others for me: when I walked into our living room and saw an utterly unknown face on the woman I loved, the woman I had married, the woman I thought I knew. It was quite a moment, and I wasn't up to it. Knowing myself somewhat better now means trying not to know as much as I once thought I did—especially when I look into a woman's face or see my own in the mirror. I try to accept my ignorance and go on from there. Some insights are leaps and some are retreats, but when it comes to love (or even romance), I try to avoid insights. Because they take you out of that moment when faces reveal themselves. To be in the moment, to be present, to look at the face, however much I still fear the unknown—that's what I ask of myself, on my good days.

On my bad days, I'm as bad as ever. But those bad days don't come often anymore, because of what I carry. I'm happy to owe that to anything, even divorce. Still, that doesn't make the past anything but what it was, what it is, what I carry.

A HEART GONE MAD

One Man's Tale

of Love and Divorce

BY *Luis J. Rodriguez*

GROWING UP in a family split between Catholic mores, Mexican Indian traditions, and the philosophies of an intellectual, semi-atheist father, divorce was an abstract, if not an absurd concept to me as we tried to settle in an unsettling world.

Ever since leaving Mexico for Los Angeles when I was two, my family had lived an urban migrant's existence. Instead of following crops, my dad pursued factory work, construction jobs, door-to-door sales, and teaching positions until he ended up as a laboratory custodian at a community college.

My mother cleaned houses, sewed clothes, and took care of strangers' children when she wasn't struggling to be the spiritual and physical center of the household.

I went to eight public schools that spanned a wide geographical area from South Central L.A. to the San Fernando Valley to the San Gabriel Valley.

Despite these dislocations, my father and mother stayed together—for more than forty years—until my father's death in 1992. They loved each other. Sometimes they didn't.

But divorce? No way.

However, the four children they bore did not have the same experience of marital longevity. For us, moving from one side of the Mexican–U.S. border to the other was the first and most significant change in our lives and would prove to be the catalyst for later disruptions.

My father's first children—whose mother died in childbirth—were either raised in Mexico or never left; in turn they maintained fairly steady marriages. My oldest half-sister Seni was married for forty years until her husband died of cancer three weeks before my father did. My half-brother Alberto had nine children and never divorced, even when the family lived in extreme poverty near a toxic waste dump in Chihuahua. My other half-brother Mario, who also never left the old country, managed to stay with his family for many decades.

The American-raised children fared differently.

My older brother Joe was the first to marry and the first to divorce. He later married again. My sister Ana married at a young age; some twenty years later she divorced. My sister Gloria had an early marriage that ended in divorce. She then remained single for many years, raising three children by herself, until one day in church she met a decent hardworking truck driver, whom she later married.

Even my two nieces, Seni's oldest daughters, who were practically raised alongside us, married and divorced at a young age.

Divorce not only became tangible for my immediate siblings, it appeared inevitable. I suppose they were becoming "good" Americans: converted Protestants, owners of suburban homes—and divorced.

Mexico had become a long-lost dream for my parents' youngest children. Never fully integrated into U.S. society, we still endured the malaise of modern U.S. culture, including divorce.

Divorce, of course, is not our whole story. But in examining divorce in the Rodriguez family, I have to address the impact that geographical changes, economic instability, and cultural shock has had on a working-class Mexican immigrant family trying to survive in the latter half of the twentieth century.

These factors also affected my own marriages. Since 1974, when I got hitched for the first time at the age of twenty, I have been officially married three times and have lived in sexual partnership with two other women.

It must be said—looking across the healing expanse of time—that I don't hold any serious resentments about my divorces. All my "wives" have been extraordinary people. They have been beautiful and loving. I suppose I've been okay, too, although I have not always been as patient and understanding as I should have been (don't get me wrong, these women have had their share of hang-ups).

I've also had the symptoms of a "bad news" guy: I have an addictive personality; I have been impulsive; I have misused drugs and alcohol. But most of all, I raged, a kind of killing rage that crippled many a decent relationship (including, at times, with my own kids).

The rage stemmed from a difficult childhood in the

83

❏

by

LUIS J.

RODRIGUEZ

streets of Los Angeles—including an abusive older sibling, abusive teachers and police, and the social stigma that claimed Mexicans had no great social value and little hope. From the age of eleven, I responded by joining street gangs, getting involved in violent acts and robberies, sniffing toxic sprays, and using heroin.

Today I see a change, although I still have a long way to go. I no longer get high, fool around, or play games. I still lose control of my emotions, though—sometimes, but not often, posing a danger to those around me (who are usually the ones I most love).

I have been married to my present wife, Trini, for eight years, the longest I've ever been with anybody. Over these years—I'm forty-two—I have sought help through therapy, retreats, recovery programs, youth empowerment work, and, especially, by writing.

I now feel I can see the intricate threads that have made up my relationships and try to understand the patterns of a heart gone mad.

AFTER A turbulent period, I seemed to have been "saved" at the age of eighteen, to the point that I began a new life on a completely different plane.

I worked in factories, which kept me from getting into any more trouble with the law. I married, had children, and got involved with a revolutionary cadre organization. I had purpose. I had vision. I had a plan. What could go wrong?

By the time I was twenty-three, everything had fallen apart. My first wife, Camila, an East L.A. woman with her own history of abuse and abandonment, had left me, taking the kids and everything I valued. Our marriage lasted a hard three years—including steel mill work that often required sixteen-hour days, layoffs, welfare and unemployment lines, study circles, community organizing, and boozing with my fellow hard hats. For Camila, it was diaper changes, dirty laundry, crying kids, and many boring days. She left, saying she couldn't take it anymore.

Soon after, I began drinking heavily again. I wanted to die again. I went from job to job. Affair to affair. I messed up in my community activities. Sometimes I couldn't even stand to see my children, and even once almost hurt my oldest son in a drunken rage.

I did things that people talk about, but you never think it's "me" they're talking about. For example, I once visited my kids, in a beer-induced stupor, and peed into my daughter's toy box, thinking it was the toilet. It was pathetic. I hated myself. I had friends, sure. Some of them stood by me, especially my *compadre* Tony. But I knew I was falling deeper into a hole. Nothing seemed to be working.

I realize I had idealized Camila. After all, she had been part of my salvation. Regardless of my irreverent adolescent years and the sundering of my siblings' marriages, I actually believed in some age-old concepts: Marriage was forever; love would never die; the people closest to you could never betray you. I gave up hurting people in street violence in order to believe in something again—some of which was expressed in what I thought was a lifelong commitment to Camila.

Of course Camila and I were too young; a frighteningly cute woman, born in Mexico but raised in East L.A., she was only a couple of months out of high school when we married. For the period we were together, she was pregnant much of the time (with my son Ramiro and my daughter Andrea). We moved around a lot; when Camila and I broke up we were living in a depressed section of Watts.

The breakup was devastating. It involved affairs with other people. There were excruciating shouting matches. Once—after she had gone out with a mutual male friend of ours—I even sat on the back porch with a loaded shotgun, thinking in a fury-filled mind that I would kill the mother of my kids! It was insane. Fortunately, we stopped the madness before it went too far.

After floundering for a few years—it was the disco age, and I danced and danced—I seemed to get a sense of direction again. Then 1980 came, a new decade for a new life. I pursued my long-held dream of writing. I went to night school. I participated in writers' workshops. I struggled for and got a slot in a journalism training program.

My life began to have meaning again—as if waking from a bad dream. I had a reason to greet each morning and not lose it. This new energy kept me mostly sober, strong, and happy. I began work as a daily newspaper reporter in San Bernardino, California. I looked healthy (I worked out with weights and jogged every day). I drank, but it wasn't the same sloppy kind of drunkenness as before. I had new friends, this time professionals, educated and as motivated as I was.

But I was lonely. I fell in and out of love (it seemed like it happened at every bus stop, at every cantina). A biker-cowgirl former prostitute and her two small children eventually moved in with me, although this only lasted a few months (her husband was a prison escapee; she wasn't worth getting clobbered for). I had long-distance romances with women in San Francisco, Tucson, Denver, and New York City—including a married Puerto Rican from the Bronx.

Then Deborah came into my life. She, too, was a journalist. She was also an aspiring actress and a singer. In time she would appear in local plays and a segment of a nationally broadcast soap opera; she even tried to be one of those bathing-suited models featured in *Jet* magazine.

Deborah. A beautiful black woman. Loving her was easy. In late 1982, we married in front of a justice of the peace in Los Angeles.

But my rage surfaced again.

I tried not to drink around her, since Deborah was not about that. But the alcohol actually mediated much of the anger—which could arise without warning. I spent a lot of time away. Although we tried to have kids, it didn't happen. Once, after a working trip to Central America, I came home to find Deborah's possessions had disappeared and Deborah was long gone. She had left me.

Trying to work things out proved difficult. Her older brother, a college professor, talked to me. Deborah's parents came all the way from Massachusetts to help us resolve our differences. I was angry at Deborah for "giving up on me."

One night, Deborah came by the house, I suppose to try and work things out. Instead, I figuratively shut the door in her face. A door of deceit and shame. Oh, I let her into the apartment all right. But an old friend of mine was in the living room, a drinking partner. I will call this person Elena; she was a street-wise friend who lasted through several affairs and a couple of marriages.

Deborah stood by the doorway, her hands trembling, perhaps trying to deny what was in front of her eyes— her estranged husband dancing and laughing with another woman. Later that night, leaving Deborah alone in the apartment, Elena and I went to her house and made love.

The fact was our expectations were not in sync: I wanted to travel, to work more hours, to be on the road. Deborah wanted me to have a nine-to-five job, to be home for dinner. To be home. But I didn't deal with this in a healthy way. A few weeks after that incident, Deborah moved in with me again, but then a few months later I fell for an old friend of mine, Yolanda, a Mexican-Colombian who had just separated from her husband. A month after I left Deborah, I moved in with Yolanda and her five-year-old daughter.

WHAT I remember most was the sound of the morning birds and the way the sun burst through the trees and rooftops at dawn. I had not slept for several nights. I was in a stone funk. This had happened before: when Camila had broken off with me, and I seemed to be floating in the world, like an emotional demon with wings but no feet—and no ground to land on.

The cause this time was Yolanda telling me she didn't want me anymore. I had just returned from three weeks in Miami, where I was on an assignment as a public affairs associate for an international public employees' union (my journalism career by then had been reduced to freelance status). Something had changed. I got the sense that I had become an intruder in Yolanda's house, caught between a daughter who missed her father and her mom who probably missed him too, although this never became clear to me. Of course, I didn't want things to change. But there seemed to be nothing I could do about this.

I felt like running and running, it didn't matter where, to let the pain, the anger, the destructiveness leave my bones. I had again idealized a woman. Yolanda was "perfect." She was intelligent. She had a career (a genetic counselor for a social agency in South Central L.A.). She was a guitarist and a great interpreter of Mexican ballads. She was also strikingly attractive, with long black hair that swam across her back, fine Latina features, and skin the color of watered dirt on a Yucatán afternoon.

Losing her meant losing part of my soul. But I had recast her in an unreal image, and this wasn't fair—to her or me. It's like that old adage of falling for "the Knight in Shining Armor" that some women are accused of doing. In this case, I was falling for a Venus on a Veranda. This is too much to place on any person, especially when the reality hits that the shining armor is tarnished and the veranda is partly crumbling.

Eventually Yolanda came back—and I was happy. We bought a house with a swimming pool on a hill in Northeast L.A. I would go on other trips, to do stories from Mexico, for example. But I would return more angry, more demanding, making it hard for anybody to appease my emotional needs. I reverted to what I felt as a youth, a belief that nothing could really work out right.

In fact, I lost trust, I lost faith that Yolanda would stick it out. It wasn't just about her, but my perception about relationships in general. They would not last. So, in effect, I would destroy them.

In a year's time, we had had it. Although there had been no children, and we were not officially husband and wife, Yolanda and I had a house and sometimes that could be as binding a force as any other between couples.

In order to leave—the particulars of which I had learned to master—Yolanda and I agreed to let her keep the equity in the house; she gave me the little bit I had invested (she put in much more of her own life, including the money from the sale of a previous house she owned).

I moved into a basement apartment in my brother's house in Boyle Heights, where I had once stayed while dating Deborah. As before, I felt "out of it." I exercised, again working out and jogging around Hollenbeck Park. I began other affairs, some with women in the bars of Tijuana and downtown L.A.

And I cried a lot.

Nothing appeared to mitigate the overwhelming loneliness—not even Elena, who stopped coming around after a serious argument. I drank too much, alone in my room, with the TV on, surrounded by paper plates of half-eaten burritos. I tried to write, I tried to get back into the swing of things, but I found myself feeling that pull in my gut, an emotional drainpipe that seemed to suck everything in.

My way out this time took the form of leaving Los Angeles altogether when I was offered an editing position in Chicago. In May of 1985, I packed my most important possessions into the back of a Nissan pickup and a U-Haul trailer. Along the way, I visited friends in the California desert and in Phoenix. I drove for miles and miles; just out of Denver I went almost fourteen hours straight. I weathered some intense thunderstorms in the Midwest, once having to pull beneath an overpass when the downpour threatened travel.

Most of the time I thought of Yolanda, her image haunting me. I sang songs to her. I called out her name. Sometimes I stopped to write letters I never sent. Whatever "bad" she may have done—such as not picking me up at the airport because she "forgot," or making dinner plans for herself and her daughter, but not for my kids or me—I only missed those times when she gently moved my hand across her breasts, when she sang her ballads with a guitar on her lap while I blacked out on tequila, or when she lay with me in the backyard late at night alongside the blue lights of the swimming pool.

Again, I had turned Yolanda into a figment of my imagination. I didn't miss Yolanda the real person (who had her bad days, let me tell you). I missed the dream.

The fact is all these women were hard-working and ambitious, with needs that I often couldn't see because I was too concerned with my own needs, my own delusions, my own obsessions. Abusive drinking, for example, is one of those self-centered things that rips at relationships. I was also very impatient so that when they didn't come through as I thought they should have, or when they had other interests other than my own, or, for example, when Yolanda wanted to spend time alone with her daughter, I often felt left out and unwanted. It was me or nobody. All or nothing. I was an insecure, regular-looking dude who "found" his worth in a woman's eyes, instead of recognizing the innate value I already possessed.

After several days crossing the country—taking my time or driving as if there was no tomorrow, days filled with doubt, hope, backtracking, excitement, and fear— the jagged Chicago skyline appeared on the horizon one humid afternoon.

Chicago. Now there's a city! The skyscrapers were taller than any I had ever seen (taller than any in the world at the time). The housing in the neighborhoods I encountered was largely brick or old graystone. It was usually three-story flats, in varying architectural shapes, with soot on the walls and years of trash in the yards. There were people everywhere, on stoops and corners, thawing out from the winter freeze a scant few weeks before. Fire hydrants with rubber tires wrapped around the openings blasted relief to kids burning under the scorching sun. The city thrived. The city smirked. The city played hopscotch and "bones."

I was thirty years old. My kids were back in L.A. All my romances and jobs and rampages and drinking partners and bloodshot nights and fistfights and disco clubs—all had been left behind for a new start, a new time. A new place.

The pickup/trailer, dusty and dented, clambered along the potholed streets of Damen Avenue to an address I had in the city's West Town community. In a few miles, I went from Mexican neighborhoods to black to Italian to Polish to Puerto Rican. Chicago: a city that won't let you forget it's a city (in L.A., sometimes, you could).

I ended up staying in the back room of a Humboldt

Park flat, where I placed books, clothes, music tapes and albums, scattered writings, photos, and clippings, packed in their boxes, around my mattress that I had spread across four cinder blocks.

One of my neighbors in the building was Trini. If anyone could make me forget the losses, it was her, formerly of the Pacoima barrio of the San Fernando Valley, one of eleven siblings in a Mexican family that once followed the migrant stream to California.

A gypsy like me, Trini also landed here to contribute at another level of commitment to revolutionary change as editor of the bilingual *Tribuno del Pueblo,* presently published by the League of Revolutionaries for a New America. She was a stable, smart, and giving person. Her beauty was unique, with Mediterranean/Native American features that could captivate any person, male or female. She had problems like everyone—and thank God not like mine—and I still learned to love her.

With me, Trini endured and stayed. She inherited a troubled boy and a quiet but unsure girl—my kids from L.A.—and a raging, poetry fool.

She endured my late nights reading in bars and cafés; my numerous jobs and long hours; my many agonizing seances of writing, or rather writhing, a poem or story out of the wells of my desperation. She endured my outbursts. My gnawing emptiness. She struggled and also wept. She methodically and consistently met all the challenges. And she challenged me to do the same.

In 1988, when my third child was slowly growing within her, Trini and I married in Kenosha, Wisconsin. After that, so much burst out of me: books, ideas, hustles, performances—and lots of poetry.

My oldest children, Ramiro and Andrea, were

reconciled with me before going off on their own (by mid-1996, my third grandchild had been born). My two youngest sons, Ruben and Luisito, were able to live in a household that nurtured, provided, and cared for them.

Not everything was rosy, but that's not the point. In late June of 1993, I stopped drinking. I also quit all my peripheral jobs, including a news-writer position for an all-news radio station, to concentrate on my lectures, workshops, conferences, and writing.

Trini has become my *compañera*—a true companion in politics, work, and love (she presently coordinates and organizes my tours). She quit her full-time job as a Spanish interpreter for the courts and curtailed her duties at the *Tribuno del Pueblo*. This arrangement also allows Trini and me the time we need to be with our boys.

I've also learned to accept the unique qualities of the various women in my life, finally realizing that when Camila left me, breaking my heart in the process, it was my anger, drinking, and working late and long hours at a steel mill that had already pushed her away from me. Or that my selfish quest for writing glory kept me aloof from Deborah's hopes for a child and a family. Or that my emotional ups and downs forced Yolanda to get off the roller-coaster ride before it came crashing down on her.

Even with Trini, there have been rough times: breaking up, returning, slamming tables, and almost coming to blows. But at present, seeing me through some of the hardest times in my life (there have been some scary health problems—despite my best efforts to work out, I gained a lot of weight over the years), Trini is still there, and I have to be there, too—including controlling whatever emotional responses remain from my early years (largely by not drinking). I never wanted to be in so many arms, so many beds, so many lives, lost and searching and needy and mostly blinded by alcohol and ego. Divorce for me has been a war zone. An extension, I suppose, of the war zone in the streets. I'm sure it has been this way for my brother and sisters, who, despite setbacks and mistakes, have managed to establish decent families.

In the end, as my parents demonstrated, we have not given up on love. Somehow, for me, at the farthest reaches of my mind, I believed that love would assert itself, even when the evidence before me suggested otherwise. That even with the sleepless nights and painful mornings, my divorces were not really the end, but the foundations for new beginnings.

I've learned that to partake in a deep, monogamous, and intimate love—bound by willing sacrifice and realized through struggle, courage, and maturity—means appreciating the limitations both social and personal that exist between two people.

It also requires doing what has to be done.

Divorce may be part of this. It may not. But I don't believe it should be the first option. That should go to commitment and love. My experience suggests that too often we let divorce intervene in the relationship before the commitment is finished.

A couple should reach the point where they can truly see themselves at their worst and best and still be strong (and strong enough to guide and influence another generation to safe passage and growth). Love is a relationship. It can't exist when only one person loves and the other is playing at it, when only one is committed and the other is not sure. Divorce should not be about severing relationships, but about letting two people go their way who for whatever reason can no longer relate.

Dare to love. Dare to be loved. Dare to lose. There's no other way to live.

96
❑
A Heart
Gone Mad

PANDORA'S BOX

BY *Jonathan Rosen*

PANDORA'S BOX was a book. Growing up I knew, from an early age, that my mother was a writer. I never read any of her books but I handled them often, always with reverential awe. Who knew what lurked beneath the covers? I peeked inside once and read a strange name I did not know. I peeked inside again: A man and a woman, naked in bed! I turned the page and read a sentence about sadness that frightened me because it came from my mother, who was a cheerful woman.

Even without reading them there was plenty about my mother's books to confuse and attract and alarm me. I found myself most drawn to her first novel. The biography on the back of that book noted that my mother lived with her husband and daughter in New York City. Where was I? The book had been published, of course, before I was born, but that seemed a poor excuse. I read that account over and over, and it was like looking in the mirror and finding that I had no face.

Even stranger than the biography that appeared on the back cover was the name that appeared on the front. Sandwiched between my mother's first name and her last name—my last name—was a name I did not know. It wasn't my mother's maiden name and it wasn't my mother's middle name. Like the invented names I'd glanced at inside the book itself, it was entirely unfamiliar.

I asked my mother many times about that name, and she always told me the same thing. It was, she said, her writing name. She told me that many writers had invented writing names. Mark Twain wasn't a real name. And George Eliot was really a woman who had chosen a man's name.

But why, I demanded, didn't her writing name appear on her other books?

I got tired of it was all she said.

And then one day, when I was thirteen years old, I learned that my mother had been married before. She had been very young at the time, the marriage had lasted only a few years, and there had been no children. Nevertheless, the news had a shattering effect on me. I felt, and there is no other word for it, betrayed. I walked around the house in wounded fury, almost physically sick. My life felt oddly over. Nothing had changed, but everything was different.

And yet, for all my surprise, the news confirmed things suspected but unpursued. There had been clues. For one thing, there was my mother's wedding dress. This was a simple black-and-white sleeveless gown that hung in her closet. I'd noticed the dress for the first time while looking for the air gun I'd been given for my sixth birthday by a girl who loved guns and whose parents, unlike my own, allowed her to play with them. Occasionally, hunting for the gun, I would become sidetracked by the dress. I sometimes went into the closet expressly to visit it.

Peering into my mother's closet created the same frightened excitement as looking into one of her books. The dress hung there like a character—unknown, alluring. I knew there was something unusual about the dress, though I couldn't have said that it was because wedding dresses were white while this one was black and white. In fact, precisely because of that dress, I thought the color of a wedding dress was a matter of personal preference. The white ones seemed ostentatious to me, a sign of poor taste.

Until I learned about my mother's first marriage. Then I thought of that dress, and of the pictures of her in the dress. Was this why my parents' wedding had been so small?—a sparse gathering of about ten people. I thought I had answered that question long before: My father's parents had been murdered in the Holocaust. The small, somewhat somber gathering seemed appropriate to an orphan's wedding. But what if it wasn't the tragedy of Jewish history but something far more ordinary, something far more American? Something trivial and yet, confusingly, something that seemed as mysterious as anything I had ever imagined.

I thought, suddenly, of the name embedded inside my mother's name—the writing name that appeared on her first book. I whispered it to myself with new understanding. O my prophetic soul!

Hamlet sees his father's ghost and learns he's been

99
❏
by
JONATHAN
ROSEN

murdered. It wasn't my father's spirit I'd encountered, but the spirit of the man who might have been my father. And if he *had* been my father, then I, as I knew myself to be, would never have been born. *I* would have been the ghost. The news was devastating—my first visit from Death—but it was also darkly exciting.

All the hidden sins that I imagined sleeping in my mother's books flooded now freely out into open thought. Who was that couple I had glimpsed having sex in one of her novels? What else went on in there? And in real life? It was no longer possible to separate imaginary events from real ones. I viewed my mother's first marriage as nothing less than infidelity—never mind that she hadn't met my father yet, and my sister and I had not been born.

Compounding my sense of betrayal was that the information had been kept secret from me until I was a teenager. Who knew what other secrets lurked in her past? If this was possible, anything was possible. Who *was* she? And perhaps, because I could not bring myself to pursue that question, I began to ask myself another question: Who was *he*? I decided to find out.

These days it is fashionable for adopted children to go in search of their biological parents. Children abandoned at birth spend years hunting for their real fathers. I felt compelled to hunt for the man who really wasn't my father. I had very little to go on. Interviewing my parents directly was out of the question. I had to sleuth it out on my own.

Little by little, a few crumbs of information came my way. I knew his name and immediately looked him up in the New York City white pages—something I continued to do, without success, for several years. I knew he was a musician. My grandmother, who had been friends with the man's family, told me dismissively that he had been "an arranger," which made him sound like a gangster, a man who fixed fights and orchestrated payoffs rather than musical scores. He had given, she told me, piano lessons to earn money. My mother also played the piano, but had his fingers once tickled the keys of the upright in our living room? This thought obsessed me briefly until I remembered my parents had bought the piano so that my sister could take piano lessons. This realization only compounded my suspicions. *Was* she my sister? Question one thing, question everything.

One day, while visiting my grandmother, I was looking through family photos, hoping to find some evidence of the phantom nonparent who had so unfairly displaced my own kind, flesh-and-blood father in my imagination. My grandmother had a lot of photographs and I was determined to sift through all of them. Here were the real characters, living and dead, who figured in my mother's life. They were mere ghosts compared to what I sought, though it seemed unlikely that what I wished to find would in fact appear. But then I found it, flattened at the bottom of the box.

It was a large photograph, about eight inches high. There was my grandmother, a broad hat with feathers on her head, beaming proudly at the camera. Beside her stood my mother in a beautiful white wedding gown— "Of course white," my grandmother said, surprised. "It was from Henri Bendel and it cost a fortune." My mother's veil was swept back. She was lovely, young and radiant. And there, beside her—a jagged edge, running the length of the photograph.

My grandmother, it turned out, had torn all the wedding photos in half after the divorce.

I had found the answering image to the small snapshots of my parents' tiny wedding, and it proved worthless. Certainly it taught me nothing about the man who had been on my mother's left, though it did teach me something about my grandmother, who, when I asked her why she had done it, answered curtly, "What the hell do we need him for?" It also taught me something about the pain my mother must have suffered after her separation. A world of fear and anger and disappointment was suggested by my grandmother's crude surgery. Understanding was not. But this information was small consolation. It was the missing man I was looking for, the man who had Houdinied his way out of the photograph, and out of my life.

There was, however, one small piece of evidence my grandmother had not been able to destroy. Examining the photograph more closely, I discovered, resting on my mother's shoulder, a man's hand. The hand vanished into a sleeve and the sleeve vanished behind my mother and then into the engulfing abyss of the torn half of the picture. But there, irrefutably, was his right hand. The hand of her husband.

I was, at about that time, learning about Darwin's theory of evolution in school, and I remember thinking that this hand was as shattering as anything Darwin himself might have described in *The Descent of Man*. The hand offered the least complete but somehow the most persuasive piece of evidence I'd encountered. I had unearthed a fossil in my own backyard.

The fact that, as a species, we share an ancestor with monkeys has never troubled me. I accept that we are descended from tree-dwelling, long-tailed creatures who gradually came down to earth and learned to walk upright. It's the intermediate half-humans that haunt my imagination: Australopithecus, Cro-Magnon, Neanderthal. They walked upright, clothed themselves in skins, knew fire, made tools. Where are they now? Did they have souls? Could they love? Were they part of the plan? A rough draft? A trial run? Or are they proof that there is no plan? Who were these other men so neatly excluded by the story of Adam and Eve? When their bones began to turn up in the fossil record, a great melancholy overtook civilization that has never left it.

To this day the slow dawning of evidence that gradually persuaded Darwin of our imperfect, primate origins has remained joined in my mind to the discovery of my mother's misted past. Perhaps divorce has done to the present age what Darwin did to the previous one. It has introduced a sad awareness of chaos into the ordered world we've tried so hard to persuade ourselves we belong in. The idea of perfection, that we get it right the first time, that we are as we were meant to be, has been destroyed.

That's how I felt when I learned about my mother's first husband—the early man who once walked through her life. What was my relationship to him? What did he tell me about my mother? About myself? Under the neat lawn of my family's quiet suburban house, I'd dug up irrefutable evidence of the random nature of my own existence. I might have had a different father, and if I had, I would have been a different person—or I would not have been anything at all.

These troubling thoughts, the melancholy of human evolution and the mystery of individual development, are inseparable, for me, from the encompassing mystery of writing. All writers have a third hand, invisible and wedded to an earlier self—a self bound up with childhood and with our human beginnings a million years ago. The hand beckons from the deepest past and points toward the furthest future. It lifts the veil on what is hidden but hides the face of what is found. It creates order but discloses chaos. It disguises with art while it reveals through imagination. It is the hand I found in the torn photograph and that has somehow become my own. It is the hand that guides the pen. The hand that writes these words.

In the biblical story of Jacob and Esau, the hand is literally an instrument of deception. Jacob wraps his smooth hands in goat skin to fool his blind father into believing he is Esau, the hairy, wild but beloved eldest son. The deception works. Isaac gives his blessing to Jacob, thinking he is Esau. "The voice is the voice of Jacob," Isaac says, "but the hands are the hands of Esau."

Hands are not to be trusted. Appearances deceive. And who is the author of this biblical deception? Jacob's mother, Rebecca. She knows Isaac, her husband, can be fooled and she knows what will fool him. She is the one who tells Jacob what to do and what to say. Isaac is wrong when he says "the voice is the voice of Jacob." It's really Rebecca's voice, whispering lies. Rebecca is the author of that whole drama of deception, the first real writer in the Bible.

My own mother, also a writer, had for me something

of Rebecca's mythic power. That my mother was a loving parent and a devoted wife did not disturb the deeper notion, enhanced by the discovery of her divorce, that she was at the same time a master of duplicity. After all, she had two husbands and I hadn't known.

Perhaps one reason I have not read my mother's books is that I wished from an early age to be a writer myself and feared that her fictional voice would prove somehow primary, the voice, as well as the body, that literally engendered me. I feared that behind my own inventions would be my mother's voice, whispering. *The voice is the voice of Rebecca.* When your mother is a matriarch of invention, the road to patriarchy is indirect and fraught with deceptions of its own.

But perhaps my reluctance to read my mother is something even more primary. There is an oedipal intimacy between Rebecca and Jacob, teaming up to fool Isaac. Have I avoided my mother's fiction because I wished to preserve the safe and sexless emblem of a loving parent? To read her fiction would be to open Pandora's box, to get between the covers, as it were, with a woman whose imagination was nakedly revealed.

The imagination is promiscuous. A writer, while writing, can be descended from other people, married to other people, in love with other people. A writer can *be* other people. And so, for that matter, can anyone, if only in their dreams. It is a frightening discovery. That my mother really did possess a secret life—as all parents do—merely gave the discovery added force. Nothing teaches children about our capacity for deception, for multiple selves, like divorce.

When I married my wife I persuaded her to have a

small wedding in my parents' house. Perhaps I wished our wedding to resemble, in its modest intimacy, my mother's second marriage. I wanted to insure that it would be the permanent one, the lasting one. I wanted to thwart the random hand of chance.

We were married only five years ago and yet I look at our framed wedding picture as if it were an artifact from some past life. There is about this picture as much mystery as in the torn photo I found in my grandmother's apartment. Our photograph is whole, no angry hands have divided us. We are joined lovingly in that picture and in life. And yet I feel the uninvited image, the shadow of the third hand, conjured by the darkening power of the imagination.

I look again and see that the shadow has passed— the hand is my own and the woman in the picture is my wife. Why then, looking at that picture, do I feel a terrible ache, as if she were indeed lost to me—though I know, at any moment, she will walk through the door? Perhaps it is because the ripped image lurks behind the whole one, and with it the knowledge that the slow pull of life, as well as the lightning gash of accident, can tear things in two. Or perhaps it is because even a marriage built on love ends inevitably in the terrible divorce of death.

The picture frightens me. And so I imagine that some future child of ours will look at it one day. I see him holding this photograph in his hands, marveling at the beautiful woman in the white dress, and wondering who that man beside her really is.

FIDELITIES

BY *Edward Hoagland*

TWO-TIME LOSER'' was the term for somebody twice divorced, in the argot of my youth. Earlier, under my parents' roof, divorce had been considered simply unthinkable. They knew no one who had been divorced because they cut off contact with anybody who had, and for the three hundred years that family records or tradition existed, no ancestor had found such a step necessary. You were a "quitter," as my father said, if you did, and in his world of corporate lawyers your career would suffer subtly, like that of problem drinkers, or people who took crass advantage of financial inside information, or men who because of sexual deviance or indiscipline were said to "live below the belt." Divorce might indicate psychological unsoundness or just a lack of follow-through. An Exxon colleague of my father's who divorced his wife to marry his secretary was exiled from Rockefeller Center to a sort of stringer post in Saudi Arabia because if *that* contract, "till death do us part," was violated with impunity, what did it say about the person's probity in lesser agreements and partnerships?

Of course, so clear a sense of right and wrong has long since blurred. "Quitter," "loser" aren't terms you hear thrown around, any more than "probity." Many people marry temporarily or try alternative lifestyles. "Losing" has to do with income, not integrity, but even money has begun to play second fiddle to mobility now in plenty of alert and comely people's minds. And mine was the generation, now sixtyish, that coolly oversaw this change—neither protesting nor quite yet reveling in it. The kind of integrity embodied in trusting a man's handshake for a business deal had also countenanced egregious racism directed against "jigs" and "kikes," "wops" and "Chinamen"; and thus we converts to the newfangled moral fluidity that accepted easy divorce and what in my father's day might have been called "checkered" professional careers were achieving an advance in democratic idealism at the same time.

Though twice divorced, I don't regret the narrative of my life. Indeed, I may have partly sought the first one as a means of severance from my parents. (After my sister did the same, our mother took to her bed for three days and our father effectively wrote us out of his will.) But as a college professor, I see the insidiously debilitating injuries divorce inflicts on kids. Around 1950, my first wife had been a pioneer in undergoing this lately more familiar ordeal of childhood and had acquired what I thought of as a lifelong fragility as a result, which in our marriage frightened me. On the other hand, the reason her shakiness particularly alarmed me was because it seemed to chime with what I remembered of my mother's. And *hers* could not have been the product of divorce, but rather of the angst of parents who felt stuck with each other—as perhaps my own tics and driven habits are.

Being fond of one another, we had managed an amicably static marriage for four years, and I knew our divorce wasn't strictly necessary—that in another era we might have muddled through for decades—whereas in the case of my second divorce, thirty years later, I'd grown so unhappy I knew I had to leave; I was suicidal. A marriage lasting for a quarter century has been through many stages and is a richer brew. But that first time, back in 1964, I simply believed that good novels were seized out of the empty air by living on the edge and that unless he or she was remarkably lucky, divorce was all but inevitable for a writer. Displeased with my third book and stalled on my fourth, I was hungry for a bout with grief, hysteria, or any other heightened emotion that might reinvent or invigorate me, and I didn't count my wife's occasional need for tranquilizers as a useful challenge. It was not a fair idea, but my wife, who worked at the United Nations as a statistician and was fair to a fault, paid a couple of months rent on our place on East 10th Street in New York to help me get started after she moved out. She also got involved with our landlord, a chunky young guy who had recently inherited the building (suddenly he started avoiding me, ducking quickly off the stairs if I was coming down), as I did with the woman who had been living on the floor below us, existing on "rice money," as she called her welfare payments, with her small son.

I bought the boy a fire engine that Christmas, I remember, which he hardly dared believe was actually meant for him, and upgraded my new friend's groceries and wardrobe a little, sharing life with them for a few months. Besides solacing myself, I was experimenting with the pleasures of fatherhood (I hope, carefully, because I knew I was going to move on), just as I had eight years earlier, during my mid-twenties, in seeing another unwed mother through her pregnancy and the birth of her daughter, knowing it would be a while before I felt confident enough about the course of my life to father children of my own.

My wife in the meantime forsook our Long Island–bred slumlord for more congenial UN boyfriends. The first of these was an agile, intellectual Frenchman who not only showed her she could "come" with the best of them but indirectly showed me, too, when she returned to East 10th Street on visits and taught me belatedly how to recapitulate what he had done to make it right for her. These were not lighthearted reunions and I don't want to make them sound so. Solicitous of each other, we were wobbling on a seawall overhanging more hysteria than I had bargained for. She was a dear, pure-spirited woman, and in four years we'd never quarreled laceratingly or been unfaithful sexually: So it seemed a somewhat schematic rather than a compulsive separation, and time has not proven or disproven whether it was for the best except in the sense that my books improved.

Her next boyfriend was a Hungarian diplomat. During the Cold War this provoked immediate FBI surveillance even within the corridors of the UN. She found out how many elevator operators and maintenance people on supposedly neutral territory were moonlighting as gumshoes. Others stood all-night vigils outside her apartment building when he slept over, and Eastern European voices would call me up to ask if I knew she was "committing adultery." Or were we "separated"? When she saw her lover off at Idlewild airport, a handsome blonde female operative stood next to her, striking up a sympathetic impromptu conversation and observing her tears. My wife stayed at the U.N., with some side ventures, and never remarried, though only twenty-eight when she went down to Mexico to procure our Spanish-language divorce. She'd always been the linguist in our travels, and the partner who could complement my brusque temperament with an ameliorating sense of humor. For years afterwards I dreamt about her in poignant scenarios—us hearing each other's voices and running from opposite directions for two city blocks or down a subway platform to embrace. And she made a couple of trips to Madison Square Garden to obtain mementos, like boxing gloves or a circus elephant handler's hook, that I could keep as emblems of my first two novels.

The culture of the period, however, was flux and dis-integration, egalitarian and chemical experimentation, sexual splurging and hip-hop long-distance driving, so a more limber sort of stamina seemed called for—even to somebody like me who didn't do drugs or believe that life was fashionably Kafkaesque. Bleecker and MacDougal Street hangouts in the Village, like the Figaro, the San Remo, the Rienzi, the Bitter End, the Village Gate, and the Feenjon, attracted yet intimidated or repelled me. Young women in black leotards swarmed there, and I liked the coffee and the sense of caffeine fermentation (or tumid semen), but not the acid, pot, and beakers full of carrot juice they were likely to offer you if they invited you home. *April is the cruelest month*, the Wasteland said, and their Lethe/Circe ideology that time ought to stand still accompanied but stood in contrast to the reigning nervous thwartedness which was practically obligatory in coffee bars and for which Kafka was the avatar.

But Kafka or T. S. Eliot in person might not have scored as fast at the Figaro as some hybrid of Samuel Beckett, Fyodor Dostoyevsky, Bob Dylan, Jack Kerouac, and Miniver Cheevy.

> Miniver Cheevy, child of scorn,
>> Grew lean while he assailed the seasons . . .
>
> Miniver mourned the ripe renown
>> That made so many a name so fragrant . . .
>
> Miniver scorned the gold he sought,
>> But sore annoyed was he without it . . .
>
> Miniver coughed, and called it fate,
>> And kept on drinking.
>
> E. A. ROBINSON

And, divining that a Tolstoy, Thomas Mann, Thomas Wolfe fan like me might swiftly come a cropper, I'd generally walk past without pausing, on the way to the cubicle I had rented in a loft building on Lafayette Street. Once, I did bring a woman I was totally infatuated with to the Five Spot, the jazz club on Third Avenue at St.

Mark's Place, to hear Thelonius Monk play the piano. But when she got inside, she dropped me for the bearded hipster Seymour Krim, author of books like *Shake It for the World, Smartass,* and—ouch, it hurt!—went home with him instead.

While married, I had got so used to my wife's loyalty that it was astonishing to be out in the real world again. Where she had been patient and tender with the countless delays and tiny inconveniences caused by the bad stutter I was saddled with, other people interrupted or sidelined me, turned their backs at parties—apologized to some celebrity whom I'd been introduced to inadvertently—and my nerdy and peremptory working schedule of lengthy hours was a problem because naturally nobody else wanted to adjust to it. I had landed my first teaching job at the New School for Social Research in order to create a second career and source of income: three hundred dollars that first semester. But the dilemma was a bit Darwinian because I stuttered so severely that, half minute by half minute, the students who had signed up to study with me wondered whether they should withdraw, or complain to the dean. One did, a retired businessman, and my survival as a tyro professor teetered on the mathematical matter of how long it took me to spit my words out.

But the rest of the class, who were mostly kindly women, stuck with me; and at a cumulative rate of about one grad student per semester, they also slept with me, making me less klutzy. Though I realized that, like my neighbor, the single mother—dark-haired, athletic in build, generous, gloomy, needy, deprived, and now nearly poleaxed by the fix she'd fallen into—they were not in a position of equality with me, I was vulnerable, too, barely able to talk or teach, living on $2,500 a year. I was a future essayist still trying with decreasing success to be a novelist, a nature writer still spending even my summers in the big city, a born optimist in an era of gleeful and much ballyhooed despair, a sexual late bloomer in a time of precocity when some people I knew were ejaculating in each other's ears.

I've written elsewhere of my second marriage: its ten fine years, thickened with the nectar of "raising" a child (nice word, and finally I had one of my own!), and then a nettly decade of decline. Marion was a deft, intuitive mother, and because we were late first-time parents, we were smart enough to go slow, pay attention, and savor pushing a swing, the first bus ride, ferryboat ride, birthday party, overnights with both grandmothers, first movie (*Fantasia*—too scary), first puppy, first visit to the zoo, and carrying our daughter on our shoulders back and forth to nursery school. *Sesame Street* and *Mister Rogers* are knitted into my memories of writing in the afternoons; and for brunch on Sunday we'd push the stroller to a clam bar and eat oysters on the half shell for a quarter apiece, squeezing lemons on them, standing on the sidewalk, then munch a whole-wheat Italian roll from Zito's, as we went along. The zigzag narrow streets and rhomboid little parks and playgrounds, the dusty sunlight angling across the aging stone of quirky, shabby buildings, the private-looking sauntering people who drew Hallmark cards or children's books, wrote Camel ads or radio shows, perhaps, for a living. Just as my first-marriage memories are from what is now called the East

Village, my second-marriage memories are rooted in the West Village, over by the Hudson, and neither neighborhood harbors episodes that in my mind's eye make me wish to flee the place. On the contrary, if our happiness curdled toward the end, that was not the city's fault; the city was our comfort.

The changing city: I overheard one baby-sitter we had hired threaten to toss our pink-skinned infant daughter out the window in furtherance of Black Power and the revolution. ("How would you like it if I threw you out the window?" she said.) But another woman, also African American, attempted to kneel and kiss my hand, in all sincerity, when I gave her a present, as if it was still slave time. This was an epoch when the historic notion that America should be a melting pot was being ridiculed, not just in black rhetoric, but more influentially in the wing of Jewish intellectual life to which my wife belonged. We'd married ecumenically, with the extra condiments of a "mixed" marriage—Protestant to blend with Jewish as the whole ideal was quite set up for—though against our parents' opposition. But then as Neoconservatism was invented, and the resurgent primacy of ethnicity along with it, we ran into trouble. Marion began to wish that she had gone to Israel as a girl and stayed there, where her heart was, like many of her friends. I'd started going to Africa to write a book about the Sudan, partly in a search for the proverbial Other that many of us look for, whereupon we discover that the Other is also us, "even" Arabs, "even" blacks. So we were moving in opposite directions, she finding even Wasps too much of a stretch.

I had lived some of my best years and done some of

my best work in this marriage, and after twenty-five years, a divorce is like dropping a whole houseful of glass, disastrous, irreparable. Can't tiptoe, although you try. One stumbles toward wide-open, vertiginous behavior with no rim to it, and the cheerful lawyers in the offing are employees and noncommittal. Friends commiserate about the "split," not as an abrogation of responsibility to be abhorred, but as a natural phase and pitfall. And yet the restive pain, the chalk-squeak jitters are not much mitigated by the fact that British Royals and every other disheveled celebrity on TV are doing it, or that old girl-friends may offer a bed and that the moviehouses and museums are sprinkled with crestfallen souls who are also undergoing a downsizing to bachelorhood again.

I was fifty-five when my second marriage derailed, and because of failing eyesight, no longer able to drive—not much of a catch. Again, it was an amicable separation and I was used to the daily loyalties, the old Irish bar saying that "you should go home with the girl that brung ya," of a settled relationship. So I was flab-bergasted when, after an old flame and I had arranged with a publisher to do a book together—an almanac of the seasons—she, a powerful artist of clouds and moun-tains, won a MacArthur "genius" fellowship and im-mediately stranded me by pulling out of the project. She was a "MacArthur" now. Grappling with semiblindness, struggling to read a newspaper, I sure found out I wasn't married any more.

From the cocktail shaker to the demolition derby and our blurry shifting cast of celebs, an entire range of American enthusiasms are based on agitation. My mother, born the same year as Charles A. Lindbergh, spent much of her considerable passion fascinated by un-consummated flirtations. My father—a Republican who stopped going to the Metropolitan Opera in 1955 when Marian Anderson became the first Negro who was al-lowed to sing there—voted against much social change, but rose from Kansas City scholarship boy to posh Wall Street attorney as the beneficiary of our national flux. Although he spent his last several years trying to com-pose his memoirs, he destroyed what he wrote and left me absolutely cleaned-out drawers from which to try to reconstruct and fathom his life, except for a single doc-ument in triplicate: his resignation letter to Exxon's C.E.O., accusing his superior in the legal department of having been a "sinister" homosexual. He had tried to maintain traditional standards, yet had kept it secret that his grandfather had been an infantry hero in the Civil War presumably because he himself had avoided military service during World War II. But to be mated for life was part and parcel of a wholesale fidelity, in his case working as a civilian negotiator for the NATO alliance against the Soviet Empire in Europe in the 1950s, and in my moth-er's, to the Episcopal church in suburban Connecticut. There, her crushes on the ministers fell within her pat-tern of flirting either with unavailable men or elegant dancing partners whose real tropism lay elsewhere. Many couples divorced in those days without getting divorced. They shared one house separately, just as they took care of their aged parents at home instead of shipping them to a nursing home, but not necessarily lovingly or well.

I can't imagine hating one's former spouse, but people sometimes did, when they couldn't get divorced. Singly, we're so much freer now that we can scarcely burn our bridges because we've got so few that matter, and can't become black sheep because so many alternative lifestyles are in vogue. The script for splitting up— burning up the phone wires, visceral pain, sedative pills, terrible bills, children weeping, messy lawyering, gnawing guilt, sleep lost, friends sought—is a tale oft-told, losing currency. And splitting isn't severance. Your memories aren't painted over. You may stand blinking before your next wife, stalling while you try to recollect her right name, thinking she must be the old one. And in bed at night, lacking the assistance of your eyes, left with scent and grope, plus the weird surrealism of your dreams: *Who is she?*

Generic pals—*which one?*—is that where we are headed? With jobs and neighbors it's surely happening. We shuffle along, buy, sell, sign on, sign off, shed or are shed by different people, call up texts and then erase them. The entry-level job, the early marriage, the starter house, and then, of course, you go from there. We think our moves are directed; we don't think it's Brownian motion. And individually most of us do acquire a crust of personality by our middle years. But have we partners?

ENDING WELL

BY *John A. Williams*

I LEFT. Hell, I walked out of a marriage that was fast closing my access to a world I had wanted to explore since my childhood ventures into the land of books. The world I lived in with my wife and children was circumscribed by race and history. I wanted my life to be bigger, different, even audacious. That wasn't about to happen.

I had committed some foolhardy acts earlier in my life: jumping into a deep river confident that although I did not know how to swim, the skill would come to me as soon as I hit the water; running away from home without knowing south from north or east from west; trying out for the bass viol in the school band because I loved its robust sound and not because I knew the slightest thing about music; punching the heavyweight boxing champ of the Boys' Club in the mouth because he snatched away my basketball when I was fourteen and an untrained lightweight; and in the WW II Navy challenging a bunch of armed rednecks alone because my buddies chickened out. I had the history of a fool rushing in or, perhaps, out.

When I left I was twenty-eight and considered myself a writer even though I had only locally published some poetry and a short, hip (I thought) piece of fiction. One poem had been published by a "little magazine" in New York.

We'd been married for seven years and had two sons. The seven years was not an itch. We had struggled through my going to college while working a variety of jobs and suffering a severe job-related injury. Then I landed in a position where I was obliged to wear a suit or jacket and slacks to work every day. Connie, who was content with being a mother and wife, tended the kids and did not work, except for an occasional part-time job. We lived in a new, state-built project, which had set aside apartments for veterans. It did not carry the onerous label public projects are burdened with today, and it was in very small part multiethnic—including me, there were two other black veterans—and located in a nice neighborhood. (My German teacher was shocked one day to see me walking with my son down the street we shared.)

This composition was just starting to become something of a norm for a few young black men in Syracuse, where I'd lived until I left, and where my father's family had been since at least 1803. I studied at Syracuse University on the GI Bill where I majored in English and journalism. Although most African American vets didn't take advantage of it, perhaps because they were suspicious that it was just another deception, the color-blind GI Bill was, to my mind, the first affirmative action program. Under the GI Bill, veterans could return to or begin college with the government paying for books, tuition, and a stipend for the vet and his family if he had one. The amount of education the government paid for depended on how long a veteran had served. The GI Bill provided for the education of a generation just emerging from the double whammy of the Great Depression and a world war. Ultimately, the GI Bill created a middle class able to pay back the nation in taxes.

SU sat on a hilltop above the interracial neighborhood in which I'd grown up, and which began a rapid change right after World War II to a largely black community as most of the whites began moving out. The cops called the area the "Tenderloin," with good reason. Whatever they did not do in other parts of the city, they did in ours.

Although Syracuse had long been an industrial town, few black men were hired to work in its factories until 1941, when FDR's Executive Order 8802 censured discrimination in factories doing defense work. The only black man to work for the L. C. Smith typewriter factory until then, for example, was the owner's chauffeur. It was the degree that got me out of the postwar odd jobs into that suit and a "good" job, first as a county case worker and then as a Children's Protective Service worker. I also worked as a copy writer at night in a public relations agency. I was one of less than a dozen local black men my age who had graduated college, so, in retrospect, I was in a unique position for that time and place.

Connie was attractive, vivacious, had a great sense of humor and a fantastic smile. She was an excellent mother, but not a very good cook. She loved to dance, which we frequently did to records and sometimes in the local clubs on Friday or Saturday, or when attending the doings of the Alpha Phi Alpha fraternity I then belonged to. It was the first African American fraternity, founded in 1906 at Cornell. Like nearly every black person in Syracuse, we went to church on Sundays, showing off first Darrell then Alton. (Connie continues to be a member of Bethany Baptist Church, which recently built a new home with stained glass windows created, as it turned out, by one of my friends.) And we paraded the kids through the neighborhoods, took drives to the countryside in a series of used cars we bought, and tried to save. We had married when I was a sophomore, but starting with my junior year I began, faintly to be sure, to see that we were growing away from each other. I tried to involve her in my studies, but she evinced little interest. Everything I wrote was "nice." She was settling in, secure and safe between home, church, a circle of friends, her children, and me, the possessor of that "good" job.

The "good" job often meant one white people had relinquished, usually due to the post-war New York state anti-discrimination laws; it tended to be a "trailblazing" position for an African American. The "good" job made one somewhat a hero in the community; it provided financial security good enough to obtain a higher level of credit from the stores downtown. It meant that you seemed to have a future even if you couldn't see it. The cops' favorite question if you had to deal with them was

"Where do ya work?" The "good" job allowed you to surprise them. Intrinsic to the "good" job was that it was not the manual labor black people had mostly been confined to since being kidnapped from Africa. Finally, it meant you were a man, a special kind of man.

It must have happened to many vets that, upon the return home, they were considered *men* because they'd been to a war. Wars do not, cannot, make men out of boys; the boys survive wars, if they are lucky, and continue to grow, warped or not, war being only a parenthetical episode. *Men* got good jobs, raised families, saved to buy homes. They spent little time reading anything except maybe the papers, and few had returned with the stupid dream of being a writer. In those days, even with the GI Bill, education got lost in the shuffle. This was America! You could achieve without going to college. Some men, most men, did just that. But not many of the successful ones were black. I considered myself a man among men, even as that great undergirding claim to such a title was eluding me. Connie and I never talked about it because we already knew the situation. Our destiny, manifestly, was to overcome it without dignifying it with a name.

I simply could not do it; I had to name, point my finger, and let my words make visible its form. I knew that in order to do this, my life had yet to be found, and it wasn't in that marriage. Connie had given me every sign that it was the concreteness not the untouchable essences of life that concerned her and the kids. Nothing wrong with that, but *I* needed more. As I began to position myself for the departure, Connie would ask "What's *wrong*?" I was unable to tell her that the marriage wasn't working for me, that there were other things I wanted to see, say, and do. She gave herself over to speculation, and I let her, knowing that some dreams are so stupid and selfish, so meaningless, so *embarrassing,* that you cannot explain them to anyone. There was no way I could rationally explain leaving a family and a "good" job in pursuit of something I could only vaguely define.

My own family of mother (and her new husband), brother, and sister had moved to California in 1948, and it was to Los Angeles I fled when I left Syracuse in what was to be a long separation before the divorce. Because I felt guilty as much as embarrassed, my attempts at reconciliation were feeble and few. Connie's response was always fiercely negative, as I knew it would be; I had hurt her too much. Her rejection suited me on one level, but on another, it deepened the guilt I felt over leaving the kids whom I had not deserted as much as failed as a father. Men maintained their families. Regardless, the part of me that really didn't want reconciliation was relieved. Immensely.

And, man, did I feel guilty! I had vowed when I was a teenager that I would *never* do what my father did to us. He remained in Syracuse until his death in 1990, three years after that of my mother, his first wife of four or five wives. When I did leave, I was confident that I wouldn't have *my* kids sweating over checks that never came to their mother for their needs. As the eldest kid in my family, I had often been delegated to pick up my father's child support checks from the clerk at children's court. They were seldom on time—or even there—and my mother's face would always crumble as if made from a graham cracker. Yet, damn it, I *did* do what he'd done. And Connie didn't deserve that; no mother did. In California I became completely aware of the pain I had caused, but the compulsion to leave had been greater than the will to stay. Guilt and an intellectually distanced remorse became my companions.

I carried with me to California the portable typewriter my mother-in-law had given me (she called me a mean son of a bitch when I left) and began the search for a job. My guilt multiplied with each failure to secure one. If I'd had fifty degrees, in Los Angeles forty-four years ago, they wouldn't have helped me get that "good" job that would allow me to care for my family and write. I slid into depression. At social gatherings, I was the guy in the corner. My mother often remarked on my posture: "Straighten up!" My jobs out there included being a valet-chauffeur in Beverly Hills; a writer of press releases for CBS-TV and NBC-TV—whenever one of their shows featured a black actor; a mail sorter in the post office at Christmas; and a speech writer for the executives of a small black insurance company, where I also wrote and edited the house publication. None of these deals approached my salary at the Onondaga County Welfare Department in Syracuse. But each was, as far as I could tell, honest work.

Watts in the mid-1950s was in some measure a larger version of the black community of Syracuse in its dealings with black university graduates—suspicious, testing, yet somewhere in the murk proud of the fact that you were. Blacks and whites rarely came into contact with each other on the same level in neighborhoods or anywhere else. (When my mother and stepfather moved to the Crenshaw district, the first blacks on their block, the place emptied of whites within four years.) The Los Angeles papers, the *Examiner, Mirror,* and the *Times* were just about to hire their first black reporters ever, but preferred locals to an easterner, which I guess was better than it was in Syracuse where I had regularly applied for and was denied work at the two dailies. I began to look longingly at the planes taking off from and landing at LAX. Connie frequently sent pictures of the kids. These were accompanied by cryptic notes about their health and how fast they seemed to be growing. But I noticed the changes of addresses—which layered more depression atop the guilt. While that may have been exactly what she wanted, I believe she also wanted me to remember what I was to them. So she sent pictures and I sometimes called. They were not living in sections of Syracuse as nice as the one we'd shared. She and her mother and the kids now lived together.

I scrimped and saved for a year, sending as much money as I could. Money, I knew from my own fractured childhood, went a long way toward ameliorating at least the surface hurt. Then I headed for New York City, where, thanks to a former classmate, who was into his first divorce, I soon landed a job with a vanity publishing house. My next step was a visit with my kids. We were strangers in spite of the pictures and talking on the phone. Connie and her mother were gimlet-eyed, unyielding in what I then believed was enduring hatred for me. Not only had I destroyed the family, I had also demolished Connie's standing in that small, fragile community of black women married to black college men with "good" jobs. (But only temporarily, for many people had taken her side. I was a first-class rat who had leaped into a deep river and so far hadn't come up.)

But I was drifting slowly to the surface, that portable typewriter my life jacket. In Los Angeles I was either feeling far too sorry for myself or too exhausted from the job search to write much of anything of worth. (I wrote only one story, but it is still being anthologized to hell and back.) In New York—gathering with friends from school and arguing and talking about Hiram Hayden's writing classes at the New School, writing in general, and other writers; about characters, locales, plots, techniques, and styles; about Dixieland's resurgence contemporaneous with the birth of Bebop, with Cool coming up fast—I began to get a glimmer of the world I had envisioned, that elusive, bodacious, intricate world that was not beyond being captured and analyzed in words.

Syracuse and its people, my family and friends nurtured my young existence, but not my aspirations (about which they could only guess) beyond the "good" job that enabled me to be a good family man. There had been occasions when my "Homies" called me "The Writer," knifing deeply into the hunger I was only vaguely sure I had. It was a phrase rendered without charity; it called me a fool, and I knew it; it dared me to become one. In retrospect, mine was a simple hunger: to know more than I then knew, and to set it down. But I was from Syracuse, and up to my time there, not many black people had managed to escape its contradictory history of being an abolitionist stronghold and a city that offered black men few opportunities, let alone that single, precious commodity, a "good" job.

A few teachers in school and the university, and Bill

Chiles, a supervisor at the Welfare Department, and Frank Woods of Dunbar Center had provided my feeble spark with winds gentle but steady enough to urge out a small flame. So did Annabell, Connie's mother, who had given me that portable typewriter as a token, I now understand, of her faith in my dream, though she surely could not have completely comprehended it. Connie herself had always seemed to care little about my studies and less about my writing.

Earlier, in my mother's home there had been little encouragement; food and rent always came first, and I understood that quite well, growing up during the Depression. Writing was not work; it was for a few foolish white people. So there was Paul Laurence Dunbar, Langston Hughes, Ann Petry, and Richard Wright. Big deal. What kind of *jobs* did they have? No one ever mentioned anything about a Harlem Renaissance with its small army of black writers.

In New York, however, I rushed into a new life and managed to augment my salary, which was none too generous, with odd writings, either for the networks under the same conditions that had existed in Los Angeles, or writing for what were then called the "girlie" magazines like *Dude, Gent,* and *Nugget,* which were trying to become miniature *Esquires* before *Playboy* copped most of the market. Within a year I began my first novel, brought the kids down for a few days, and began "going out." Then I asked for a raise and was promptly fired. Enough, I thought, and began a publication for ad and PR agencies called *The Negro Market Newsletter.* Of course, it was far ahead of its time and, also of course, just as it began to catch on, I ran out of what little money I had and was in the tank again. Friends commiserated. It was "the system" that was at fault, not me, and surprisingly, Connie sometimes seemed to understand. How she was able to, I do not know, but I think she knew by that time, if I had money, she and the guys would get it.

On my feet again in due course, I was able to help with the support of the kids. For a few years the rule was that if I wanted the kids to visit, I'd have to train or fly up, bring them back to New York, and after the visit, take them back to Syracuse. So I was surprised when Connie told me, after a few such bank-breaking junkets, she thought they were old enough to come to New York on their own. Connie had returned to school and had secured, for Syracuse, for a black woman, a "good" job as a bank teller. She even cashed without hesitation my personal checks. A couple of times we had drinks without strain when I was in Syracuse, and we talked about the kids and how well she was doing with them. Which she was. In fact, great.

I wasn't in a hurry to get the divorce, not because I entertained ideas of a reconciliation, but because I wanted to stay as free as I then felt. For I went out regularly, sometimes with women who themselves were divorced or separated with children—and were looking to get married again, to a writer. (Even black writers, legend had it around New York, made beaucoup bread and could lead them through glamorous lives.) The separation represented a reprieve in case I lost my cool: I could always fall back on not being divorced and weasel out of a relationship that had become too sticky.

When Connie and I did agree it was time to divorce,

we arranged that she go south for a quickie—in which state I no longer remember. I picked her up at Grand Central and brought her to my apartment in the Village to rest until it was time to catch the train south out of Penn Station. She may have agreed because she was thinking of marrying again. While I had no such plan at the time, I owed her her freedom if nothing else. I think we threw each other kisses when her train pulled out. As it happened, the divorce didn't take for reasons the lawyer was unable to explain to me, since he went out of business soon after. The next time I'd go to Mexico.

When I began publishing magazine pieces and books, some of the financial pressure I'd felt eased off. Connie, her mother, and I had become civil on the way to a friendship that was still to come. But the guys, I felt, had not forgiven me. There were those little rebellions, some sneaky, some in my face. Then I asked myself, "Why should they forgive me?" I worked on the holes in their lives, not always realizing that there are some holes that simply cannot be filled after the time for filling has passed. So I built, with their help, new structures into which I could place all the materials I could not earlier use.

Some twelve years after I'd left, I remarried, a couple of years after our Mexican divorce. (I flew to El Paso, met my lady lawyer, checked into a hotel, and taxied over to the courthouse in Juárez the next morning, one of the herd of Americans on a similar mission; I flew back to New York on an afternoon plane.) I married a white woman, and we had a son, Jeremy, two years later.

As Eva and I expected, a coolness ensued on Connie's part. Probably, I thought, not because I'd remarried, but because my wife was white. Such marriages seem unpopular anytime, but the sixties proved to be ticklish; today there are almost three-quarters of a million interracial/interethnic marriages, but back then not much that was white played well in black thinking. In addition, my sons were skittish, and I laid that to the double whammy I'd placed on them: a white stepmother and a brother. Quite quickly, however, all that flew past. Connie's attitude was soon replaced by a grudging admiration of Eva's care, concern, and love for Darrell and Alton. Anyone who cared for her sons had to be all right. She remarried a few years later.

My mother, Ola, who had remained friendly with Connie and Annabell, told me when Jeremy was born that Annabell remarked that I was too old to be having children. I was forty-two. Jeremy is now twenty-nine. I have never heard Darrell or Alton introduce him as their *half*-brother. Darrell has a doctorate and is an executive director of medical promotional services. Alton has an MFA and is a former newsmagazine editor; he now directs a writing program at an upstate New York university between novels; his third is due out this year. Jeremy graduated from a musical college and is guitarist with a top-rated band currently based in Los Angeles. He's also a music production engineer.

In her eighties, Ola told me she forgave my father for not helping very much to care for us when we were kids. This was during one of my frequent visits to see her in Los Angeles, and we were again going over our pasts in Syracuse. Her second husband long since dead, and displeased with the quality of her male callers, she confided that she got more pleasure from her vibrator than her "rackety old" suitors. Of my father she said, "He really couldn't help it, you know. There just weren't any jobs there for black men back then." I was silent. "Back then" had not been so far back after all. But I had survived, I was a writer, she told friends and strangers alike. Dumping the "good" job, which you were never supposed to do because, most likely, you'd never get another, was a grand demerit erased from her debit book; she never said it to me, but I knew it to be true. She was, in spite of everything, proud I had chosen to get an education when the opportunity was presented by the GI Bill; that had made me the first of my parents' families to go to college.

I've returned to Syracuse many times, to have a day proclaimed for me by the mayor, to read at Syracuse University, which, twenty-six years ago, gave me its Centennial Achievement medal and in 1995, an honorary doctorate. I had not gone to my own graduation in 1950; I was looking for a job in New York City that June. Clearly, if Syracuse and some of the people near me did not to my mind sufficiently nourish the dreams of my youth and young manhood, they have since more than made up for it, though I did not later need or seek such attention. My professional visits there are more to suggest to the young men and women, especially if they are black, that dreams are now more likely to be supported there than they were for me.

Four years ago I was in Syracuse to be grand marshal for the community celebration of Juneteenth (commemorating Lincoln's June 19, 1862, signing of the Emancipation Proclamation, which went into effect January 1, 1863). A bit late, I was rushing to the corner

132
❑
Ending
Well

where I could join the head of the parade. Across the street an attractive black woman waved and smiled at me, and I thought, *That's a fine-looking woman!* She was wearing a baseball cap with the legend *Breakout* on it. That was the name of Alton's last novel; he had passed out the caps to the family. How come this stranger was wearing one? The woman was crossing toward me; she must have seen the question on my face. "*Connie*," she said, her voice rising slightly. My apologies were profound and profuse. We talked briefly about the novel, and she asked after Eva and Jeremy, as she usually does, and I asked after her husband, Donald, and Annabell, then dashed on to the head of the parade, amazed that I'd forgotten what she looked like. But, in fact, it had been quite a few years since I'd seen her. It is unlikely that she holds this gaff against me.

Annabell, in her nineties, moves from home to hospital and back again. When I infrequently call to check on her mother, Connie tells me: "She just smiles when I tell her you called." So, over time and on a base of diminished pain, we "got over" to some degree. A friend calls our relationship "civilized." Maybe, but I once found myself covertly watching Darrell and Alton in their marriages to detect any signs that they might dream away, too, or that "the system" was bending them as it did me. (Jeremy's not married yet.) It gives me a great sense of ease to see that all's well, that the family breakups that occurred generation after generation seem to have ended, for me at least. (My two sisters have not been as fortunate, and my brother never married.) My sons were able to live their dreams, undaunted by "the system," far more than less.

If I had not left the first two, I know I'd never have been a writer; I floundered into the label. Connie's manner seems to indicate that she has forgiven me. The problem is, though, I still can't forgive myself. I think, but certainly can't know, that in all their relationships with me, Darrell and Alton are saying, "Hey, it's over and done. We're OK, and we love you." Quite frequently they voice the last three words, comforting me at seventy-one years old.

As for Connie, who, like me, is retired, she may yet hold reservations about me, though they hardly show. But I continue to feel that I abandoned a part of myself in order to find, what in the final analysis, may not have been the greater part at all. I continue to study "the system," alert to the harm it has done to many millions of men who have been unable to secure that "good" job to care for themselves and their families. "Family values," that political Frisbee, cannot truly exist while democracy and capitalism remain antithetical. Of course marriages fall apart, but when they do, it is often "the system" that prevents the wage earners, who need not be dreamers as I was, from bandaging the wounds they leave. As a result, millions of so-called deadbeat dads are as much victims of the conflict as their ex-wives and children.

My second marriage is thirty-two years long. Eva has been invaluable in helping me find my way through the guilt. Furthermore, as a second mother (and grandmother of four) she has quietly widened and enriched the mothering of my sons, their wives, and their kids. I could not ever have reached the friendship I share with my sons and daughters without her.

Dream lucky, be lucky, which I am.

THE

SORROW

AND THE NEED

BY *Richard Gilman*

I'VE BEEN DIVORCED twice, yet in childhood and adolescence I was deeply troubled by the very word *divorce*. On its face to get divorced was far from an obvious calamity, yet I thought of it as one. It seemed to me like a grave illness a couple had caught in tandem, or a violent, possibly fatal accident, a car crash.

I remember being shocked and alarmed at twelve or thirteen by news that an aunt and uncle to whom I was very close were getting divorced. Terrors assailed me, but I had to be silent about them, for in my family divorce wasn't to be discussed, not with the children, anyway, and my friends seemed under the same proscription, or labored under the same ignorance. The way I learned about my uncle and aunt was surreptitious and illicit—through eavesdropping one night on my parents. They were talking about the impending divorce in voices scarcely above a whisper, tones you'd use for something both shameful and catastrophic, a moral calamity—or so it seemed to me, listening in my pajamas in the hallway.

Yet so rare was divorce in the thirties and forties, when I was growing up, that along with a sense of the inimical, it carried an aura of exoticism; a divorced person had undergone a peculiar adventure or trial and bore marks of the experience, scars of survival. Divorced people were like war veterans: an American Legion of the once-married.

I gradually became aware that divorce had a lighter side, the phenomenon of the "gay divorcée," with that extra, significantly French, *e*. A word for a divorced man existed too—*divorcé,* with the accent but only one *e*— but nobody used it, precisely because a man's condition wasn't (in theory, anyway) nearly so radically changed by divorce. Some people thought of a divorced woman's "scars" as marks of a new erotic freedom, whose practices went from flirtation on up, a range of activity such as men of any social standing had always been freer to pursue. An attractive divorcée was thus expected to be a charmer, a temptress, and an air of the vaguely risqué rose from the word itself. At least this was true on that sophisticated plane of life into whose atmosphere Sunday sermons never penetrated.

But that was just it; divorcées were in the movies, the theater, the gossip columns, and I would never have thought of my aunt as a gay divorcée, even though she was extremely pretty, because to be divorced among the people I knew wasn't glamorous but meant having been injured . . . and at the same time being guilty. But what kind of hurt was it, and what was the crime?

The obvious sense was of something broken, a unity

destroyed. But what sort of unity was this, or, put differently, what did being a couple—in a more complex sense than simply being two of something—really mean? All I understood at the time was that the married couples I knew or knew about were so closely bound together as entities in my mind that considerations of blame didn't enter; a divorce was a disaster for two, the result of a helpless conspiracy.

Much later, well into adult life, I came to see that divorce was mysterious because I'd found marriage itself unfathomable. My parents' relationship, from which I naturally gained nearly all my initial ideas on the subject, was extraordinarily opaque, uncommunicative, and, I suspected but feared making conscious when I was young, loveless. Still, for all the negativity that seeped from them, I couldn't have tolerated their breaking up. Marriage, synonymous for me with parenthood and hence a kind of force or property of nature, was a given, part of the way things were, and so under a sort of tyranny of continued existence, not to be questioned in its essence.

For richer for poorer, in sickness and in health, and the rest of those words I would years later come to recite publicly, my parents had to stay together; it would have been "unnatural" for them to have separated, no matter how persuasive the emotional and physical evidence that they should. In a perspective that certainly looks perverse and grossly reactionary now, divorce was something not to be contemplated whatever the circumstances, equally a threat to what I'd thought of as the "happy" marriage of my uncle and aunt and to my parents' "unhappy" one.

Entirely unreligious at the time, I nevertheless was evidently bound by what was at bottom a religious commandment, however attenuated or remote from its source it had become. More precisely I was gripped by a taboo; divorce was a defiance of the prohibition against sundering what was considered—by whom? I suppose the powers, the gods, God—to be a necessary, if not actually sacred, unity. Divorce, then, floated in my early consciousness wrapped in superstitions, clouds of unknowing—and not wanting to know.

Once I passed from the age of statutory innocence, I rapidly shed my know-nothing attitude toward divorce, my outlook of fear and prejudice. How could it have been otherwise? Around me society was swiftly changing, the civic air increasingly open, creeds stretching and cracking, sexual cant and hypocrisy on the wane, ideals of "self-fulfillment" more and more triumphant. In such an atmosphere of repudiated authority and pragmatic happiness, someone like me had no trouble coming to regard divorce as not all that different from a change of career, a step taken if some earlier steps had turned out badly. Clear liberal thinking, the right mental stuff, told me that while divorce would likely be unpleasant, its shocks wouldn't affect anything deeper than my nervous system. That is, divorce wasn't a spiritual or philosophic problem; I was free of any lingering effects of the original malediction.

Or so I thought. But it turns out I've never really been cleansed in that way, despite the freedoms of the age—or in an oblique, unexpected manner because of them. Something about the triumph of personal "rights" and hence about my own emancipated behavior has resisted total approval and so, I suppose, kept me from full stature as a "modern" man.

I STEP BACK in memory nearly thirty years. I'm sitting in a park in El Paso, Texas, relieved at having just become legally free of a wife from whom I've long been physically and emotionally separated; now I can marry someone else. I have an idea of calling the woman I've been seeing with the good news. But I suppress this celebratory impulse because, to my great surprise, in another region I'm suddenly mourning and trembling with an obscure pain. Oh, make no mistake: As far as I can know, I'm truly in love with the new woman and long since remote from the old; I haven't any regrets or doubts. But the sorrow and the ache are there.

139
❑
by
RICHARD
GILMAN

These feelings weren't to be confused with the unpleasantness of the experience I'd just gone through, the conventional one at the time of a quick Mexican divorce: a flight from La Guardia (I'm the only man in a planeload of women aspiring to be single again), a one-night "residency" in Ciudad Juárez across the border, a perfunctory appearance before a Mexican judge, the whole thing cut-and-dried, mechanical, false. Those proceedings offended my sense of dignity; but the unexpected pang affected me in some deeper place.

MY SECOND divorcing was more abstract, with nothing more physical than a large set of papers. In the intervening years, divorce as a legal process had become much more straightforward, less tainted with lies; so you didn't have to go to unlikely warm places to get one.

For me there were other differences. My first divorce

had been mutually agreed upon, while the second, twenty years later, had been imposed against my will, its terms bitterly fought over. After the first, I was ready for a new life; while in the aftermath of the second, I was lost, not nearly so hopeful, and, naturally, being considerably older, much less resilient. Yet—the crucial point—none of these differences mattered at all to the presence, in the immediate atmosphere of being single again, of the pain or ache I've mentioned.

To characterize it as accurately as I can, it was a sadness or sorrowfulness, a mourning for something lost, accompanied by slight feelings of wrongdoing and failure, and—so fugitive I have to strain to capture it—that old sense of broken taboo. At intervals throughout my life, married and unmarried, since that time in El Paso when it first surfaced, this knot or cluster of awarenesses has reappeared.

How can I emphasize enough that this feeling had nothing to do with the realities of the marriages I was moving out of or into? It didn't in any way measure my happiness or its lack. For that matter, it's never been accompanied by any change in my conscious political position on divorce. I'm just as "liberal" as ever in this area; I still see divorce as a right and, in many intolerable circumstances, a necessity. I'm sure I'll never lose my gratitude that divorce is available, a way out, a way in: a means of leaping or squirming free of otherwise iron fate.

Still, what I've come to call the Feeling, that pang of complex sorrowfulness, persists, however infrequently it makes itself known; emerging stealthily as if it has been living in its own dimension neutralized under layers of learning and "proper" attitudes, it summons me, when it appears, not to remorse or regret for my acts but to something far more subtle and evanescent, simply—or surely not so simply!—a sense that things aren't quite right in the universe. Only during its latest visitation have I been able to pursue that further, for always before this, while I struggled for the will and courage to examine the Feeling, it would disappear. But in the last few years I've had reason and occasion to be less fainthearted.

IN 1987 IN JAPAN I met Yasuko, the woman who is now my third wife. When our intimacy began, my second divorce was long settled, just months from becoming official, but she faced the most difficult process of getting out of her own unhappy marriage. Although Japan is slowly changing, it is still maybe a generation behind America in certain ways, among which the legal and what I call philosophic position of women, especially married ones, is prominent. To put it as succinctly as possible, divorce in Japan is hard to get and tilted against the wife.

This isn't the place for a detailed discussion of the sociology of Japanese marriages, or any discussion at all of my relationship with Yasuko, except to say that it's deeply satisfying. But her arduous and often agonizing effort to get a divorce revealed to me things that are at the heart of this essay's subject. But first some background, radically foreshortened.

At twenty-nine, very late at the time for a Japanese woman to be still unmarried, Yasuko accepted a potential mate through an *omiai,* the interview process for which "arranged marriage" is a rather misleading translation. But it makes the point that she wasn't propelled by expectations of marital bliss; she'd gone soberly into the union, motivated by a desire for children and a home to go with her career as a college professor of English. Children and a vocation: a most rare combination for Japanese women in the late sixties and not exactly widespread now. But her prospective husband seemed open to it, an unusual stance which encouraged her to go ahead.

She had two children early in the marriage, worked hard at raising them, and still managed to advance in her career. Fairly soon, though, her husband, also an academic, made it known that he resented her professional life. Indeed, it became ever clearer that far from being the relatively liberated potential mate she'd thought him, he was, in fact, a fairly classic example of the conventional Japanese husband: patriarchal, self-centered, someone to whom child raising and housework were entirely alien—women's business. And beyond those generic disfigurements, he suffered from an incapacity to give her credit for her virtues and from envy of her more capacious mind. The relationship began to fill with tensions and gaps.

When she met me, about fifteen years into the marriage, they had long been emotionally and intellectually estranged, though the rift was hidden from the world under a facade of marital correctness and composure. This was fated not to last. Nurtured on American and British culture and having been a Fulbright scholar in the States, Yasuko had become creatively poised in her values and affections between East and West. Among other things, this meant, as was gradually unfolded to her, that she subscribed more than most Japanese women of her generation to the proposition that, ideally at least, marital relationships could be sources of personal satisfaction, inner blooming—rather than, at best, simple working arrangements or, at worst, instrumentalities of the maiming of self, as her own marriage had been.

We fought against falling in love—she because she feared losing her children or injuring them; I because I didn't want to be the agent of that and dreaded being an interloper in so fixed and hierarchic a culture. But finally we succumbed. We were playing it by ear, keeping things secret while she groped for solutions, when everything suddenly blew up. Her husband, prowling through her things, found a letter from me full of amorous avowals and indications that we'd met. At first he threatened to kill her, me, and himself, then alternately pleaded with and threatened her, until, unable to bear it, she left the house.

For the next few years I shuttled between Japan and the States. Of the swarm of events of that period, the relevant ones concern her anguished struggle between duty and yearning, and then her efforts to get legally free. In the eyes of the law, having begun a liaison she was to blame; only her husband's certifiable madness, demonstrable homicidal tendencies, or scandalously outrageous philandering would have given her any kind of defense. But he hadn't beaten her, hadn't played around. Ibsen's *A Doll House* had its first Japanese production in 1911 and has inspired feminists in Japan ever since, but to a much greater extent than in the West, the intellectual and moral news it brought hasn't been translated into legal changes. And so the alternately high-handed and condescending treatment of wives by many Japanese husbands has had juridical support; a case based on incompatibility, so long the mainstay of justification for divorce in the West, would be laughed out of court here.

So, too, would the concept of no-fault divorce; it's always somebody's fault, and far more often than not the woman's. So Yasuko was at his mercy, having to accept whatever terms he laid down. These were harsh indeed: He forbade their children, fourteen and ten when it all began, to see or communicate with her, demanded 90 percent of their considerable mutual assets, and most bizarrely, insisted that she swear never to see me again in Japan. The proviso was legally unenforceable, of course, so Yasuko agreed to it with—in effect—her fingers crossed.

But we had to go through much more before the divorce finally came through. In the days following her husband's discovery of our relationship, he wrote me several letters which alternated—in painfully naive English—between violent denunciations and plaintive entreaties, letters which I was at a loss to know how to answer, though I tried. A year later he sued me in a Kyoto court for what used to be called in America "alienation of affections," and for all I know may still be.

Through my Japanese lawyer, a woman as it happened, I defended myself as best I could. In a twenty-five-page statement to the three-judge tribunal I set out my case: Charged with breaking up "a happy family," I argued that it was actually deeply unhappy; besides, I didn't "break up" anything, having stepped back and waited for Yasuko's decision, prepared to accept it uncomplainingly had she chosen to stay with her husband. She wrote a supporting document describing her years of unhappiness, her efforts to stick to her duty, and the pain of being kept from her children. She also affirmed my passive role in the matter.

We learned later that the judges had been kindly disposed toward us, so repugnant had they found the husband's accusatory brief, full of self-pity and obvious misstatements, if not outright lies. But the law was implacable and recognized no inner worlds. I was found guilty, and fined the minimum in such cases of about $25,000 in yen; it was some consolation to learn that the fine could have been as much as $100,000.

But our ordeal wasn't over. Before he'd agree to the divorce, Yasuko's husband demanded a written apology from me, together with my own pledge not to see her in Japan. I swallowed hard and wrote the apology according to the formula I'd been given, added the absurd pledge, and mailed it off. A few weeks later I was told that my letter was unacceptable because I'd used stationery from Yale (where I teach) instead of plain paper. So I wrote it again. It was many months after I'd paid the fine before he finally signed the agreement; a month or two after that, Yasuko and I were married in Kyoto.

THROUGHOUT the more than four years all this took, and for a long time afterwards, my feelings toward the man were all anger and contempt. He had been so vindictive (one cruelty was to forbid the children any contact not only with Yasuko but with her family, too, which among other things meant that the children couldn't attend their grandparents' funerals), so unwilling to accept the slightest responsibility for what had happened, so generally shabby and mean-spirited, by my standards, that I couldn't think of him without spasms of revulsion. He has continued to act in ways that fan my aversion: His ban on the children's contact with Yasuko remains in force, and they, eighteen and twenty-two now, continue to obey him—she hasn't seen them in eight years.

But recently, despite all the reasons I have for persevering in my resentment and dislike, a change toward him has come over me, a lowering of antipathy, a softening of contempt. As I've come to know Japan better and—who's to say, even at my age—life a little better, I've gained a degree of understanding of the causes of his behavior, and even a narrow acceptance of it; as a byproduct—or something rather more central than that—this understanding has thrown light on the Feeling I've spoken of earlier, the sorrowfulness that for me has for so long accompanied the thought and practice of divorce.

To begin with, I've gained a sense of the two of us as being looped together in the matter. We are opponents, enemies, to be sure, yet strangely made confederates, too, for we both stand along what I think of as a fault line in human activity, the crack in the nature of things from which divorce arises.

Obviously Yasuko's husband and I came to stand along this line from enormously different backgrounds and with hugely differing stakes in the matter. To sum it up with intolerable brevity, I had come to the encounter from an America—or that part of it which I inhabited—of liberality and openness, where the shibboleths are "human rights" and "personal fulfillment," and definitions of happiness aren't in need of group endorsement. Against that, this man's Japan can be seen as harsh, feudal, "inhuman" in ways; its stress on the community, on tradition, order, and hierarchy breeds certain virtues but also rigidity, hypocrisy, and blindness—an example of which was his inability to imagine any life differently from the way he saw his own and so to have any understanding of why his wife had left him.

He had radically and, from my perspective, perversely misread the marriage. In the face of a mountain of contrary evidence, he had presented himself to the court as an exemplary husband, and one of his accusations against me had been that I'd "stolen" his wife's love, when of course there was nothing there to steal. But I've come to see that by the standards and ways of judging he'd inherited or picked up through osmosis from the culture that was how it must have seemed to him, and that all he knew now was that there'd been a violent upheaval, an earthquake, a turning of everything on its head. And so he had blindly struck out in defense of his world and his *amour propre*.

He had been taught certain things, given certain models: Love isn't a matter of intimacy or mutual consciousness, but of duty, the proper filling of places; individuality isn't a desirable condition; loyalty matters more than personal aspiration; the family counts for more than its members. As alien to Americans as some of this is, particularly in what it leaves out in its view of life, it's not contemptible. Japan's ethos is as complex as any; along with the lies and distortions and stifling of human creativity caused by its remnants of moral and physical feudalism, it continues to send out lines toward foundations, toward "seriousness" about life; it breeds gestures toward what can be thought of without embarrassment or contradiction as a sort of secular "sacredness." Some of these gestures are shortsighted and self-defeating, to be sure: The desire to protect the integrity of the family, which is at the bottom of all strictures on divorce, often results in a pretense of integrity, behind which are casuistry and force. Still, the impulse behind *that* isn't to be despised.

In a culture possessing no principle of transcendence, nothing to appeal to on the order of our Judeo-Christian tradition, ideas of good and evil have a pragmatic base rooted in the past. What's right is, largely, what the group has decided is right, in its own self-interest and not that of the separate person, which is why the kind of moral change Americans know is so slow in Japan. But that's another, much larger, story. The point is that Yasuko had done something outside the sanctioned ways, which was all her husband could see.

I DON'T HAVE to like him or respect him, and I certainly don't. But I have to respect the fact of his suffering. He and I had greatly differing experiences, which aren't to be gauged by ordinary psychological or emotional measurements. His distress—an amalgam of shock, pain, anger, and loss of self-esteem—was, in the nature of the thing, intensely personal, and, I'm sure, permanent. But for me, too, the "winner," rejoicing after the ordeal of the divorce process, in the midst of our huge, quiet happiness when Yasuko was finally free, a familiar voice said that I'd have to join him in at least a metaphysical or existential realm of sorrow, if not in one springing from actual loss.

I know that what I've been saying and have still to

say is bound to be misunderstood. No matter. I've come to see that what that knot of sorrowfulness, which has formed in me several times in the past couple of years, has been telling me all along is that there's no innocence in divorce. *Everyone* is a victim in the dimension of experience I'm addressing—not, as it's intellectually comfortable to think, simply the children involved or some pathetically abandoned helpless wife (or husband for that matter) but everyone, abused and abuser, the powerful in divorce's precincts and the weak. Divorce is necessary at times, yes, of course, but it's a necessary evil not a great unalloyed good. That it *has to be* available is precisely the source of the sadness.

Yasuko's husband, perpetrator and victim, flailing against what he couldn't understand, had made it necessary for her to seek relief and change; but I know she wishes somewhere that such relief and alteration hadn't become necessary. This wish isn't at all a threat to our marriage, for she makes it as a philosophical gesture, a recognition of the malfunctioning of our human world. There is a sense in which all divorces represent failures, of particular marriages most obviously, but on a deeper, wider level of modes of life, and of the relations between institutions—culture, society—and the ways we individually live.

I said before that when I was young the very word *divorce* alarmed me and gave me an intimation of things not being quite right in the universe. This, I suppose, is a position not very far from the idea of original sin, which, however, I interpret not as inherent guiltiness, the crude view of it, but as a disposition, a tendency toward insufficiency, inadequacy, failure. Divorce is a continual demonstration of this tendency, and to take it lightly is to diminish the dignity with which we ought to regard our relationships. To take it lightly is also to demonstrate a lack of respect or desire for moral principles that have more than an ad hoc existence. To take it too grimly, however, which is to say to forbid it (as was done for so long in Ireland and Italy), or make it an ordeal and a question of blame (as used to be true in America and still mostly is in Japan) is to lack compassion. It is also to lack a feeling for circumstance, the particularities of human dilemmas such as marriages that have grown intolerable.

Just such a lack of a sense of specificity marks the more zealous opponents of abortion, who are likely to regard divorce as being in the same moral darkness. In both cases to insist that the general must triumph absolutely over the particular—no exceptions, no nuances, none of the complications of intertwined destinies—is to be deaf to individual suffering in the interests of an abstract ruling value. Still, that value, that general principle, has its claim on us, even as we're forced to find ways to evade its many overly harsh applications. How do we pay respect to what we feel compelled so often to betray?

I can only say how I myself manage. I'm fervidly prochoice, yet I think every abortion ought to be accompanied by at least a tinge of melancholy. In the same way, I have lived with divorce, depended on it in crucial ways, owe to it much of my present happiness; yet I honor the residue of sorrowfulness it leaves behind, for not to feel such sadness is truly to be frivolous about the things that matter, and, worse, to regard failure as a form of success.

MY PARENTS' BUST UP. AND MINE.

BY *Walter Kirn*

MY PARENTS stayed together for the sake of the children. When the children were grown and settled, my parents divorced—for their own sake. My brother was twenty-five and single, studying for a graduate degree. I was twenty-seven and newly married, about to publish my first book of stories. Because Mom and Dad had decided to tough it out (twenty-nine years in all), we faced their breakup not as vulnerable kids but as self-sufficient adults. You'd think it would have been easier that way: no custody battle, no change of schools, no teenage identity crises, no visitation squabbles.

You'd think I'd *thank* my parents for their decision.

Here is what I learned, though: When the rug is pulled out from under you emotionally, it isn't necessarily an advantage to be standing on your own two feet.

———

NOTHING IS quite so shocking, somehow, as news you've been half expecting all your life.

I got the word on a pay phone, in a Salt Lake City Dairy Queen. My wife and I had been camping in the Rockies and were ready to fly home to New York City. My parents, who'd been camping with us, had already driven back to Minnesota, the state where I grew up. The trip had been tense, my parents grim and distant, but I felt I had to call them. I'd read something crazy in the local paper: A dead school friend of mine whose funeral had been a month ago (his overturned raft was found floating in Puget Sound) had turned up alive in a tiny western jail.

"Karl faked his own death!" I told my mother. "Can you believe it?"

"Walt, I'm going to leave your father. I'm moving out tonight. Our marriage is finished."

I stood there with my melting ice-cream cone. Around me families slurped milkshakes, gobbled burgers. Big, happy Mormon families, by the looks of them.

"I'm sorry," my mother said. Her voice was gravelly. "Maybe you could call your brother and give him the telephone number where I'll be staying."

I hung up the phone. My wife asked what was wrong. I hated it when people asked me that, particularly when something *was* wrong. I glared at my wife and didn't answer her. We'd been married for less than two years, not always happily, and I knew in an instant that we might not have wed if what had just happened had happened years ago. One of the reasons I'd married at twenty-five (earlier than any of my friends) was to please my parents, to make them proud of me.

"My mom and dad are getting divorced," I said.

My wife let out a sigh. Her own parents had split up when she was tiny, and this was one of the differences between us. I came from a "stable" family background, she from a "broken" home.

"It's probably for the best," she said. My wife was British, and suddenly her accent seemed maddeningly proper, almost cruel. "After seeing your parents together," she said, "I can't say I'm surprised."

"Well, I fucking am!" I shouted. "*I'm* surprised!"

In fact, I wasn't; I simply needed to shout. I went on to shout a lot that year. I shouted so much, in fact, and so crazily (often while drunk and sometimes in my sleep) that by year's end I'd be divorced myself.

Let's take the bust-ups in order, though.

Let's follow the long, branching crack from the beginning.

SOME PEOPLE grew up during the Depression, some during World War II or Vietnam. That's how they place themselves historically: as children of some great, defining calamity.

I grew up during Divorce.

Though it took two more decades to infect me personally, the plague broke out around 1973 (at least in the sheltered upper Midwest). We were living, our buttoned-down family of four, in a rural Minnesota village whose men commuted to dentist-accountant type jobs in Minneapolis/St. Paul. The town had a white clapboard general store and a hilltop elementary school. The horizon was ringed by soft round human hills. Lining the streets were towering vase-shaped elms whose interlocking boughs and branches created great leafy cathedrals of cool shade.

Two evils struck simultaneously: The elms started dying, felled by a Dutch beetle, and my friends' parents started splitting up, afflicted by a more mysterious bug. (I sensed at the time that it came from our TVs, bred during episodes of *Love American Style* and in the swanky "party" section of *Laugh-In*.) The sounds of that summer still come to me in dreams: chainsaws outdoors, bickering indoors. All the adults were quarreling, it seemed.

To an eleven-year-old, it felt like doomsday. Kids started disappearing from school, whisked away by feuding parents. For Sale signs sprouted in weed-infested yards. One Sunday morning, while selling Cub Scout candy, I rang the doorbell of a neighbor's house where I'd recently attended a buddy's birthday party. The boy's father answered, gray and unshaven, holding a gin-filled novelty glass whose pinup girl stripped naked when ice was added. Behind him, the house was scarily empty. Stark.

"Sorry, out of cash," the man said, slurring. "I'd find some loose change in the couch, except she took the couch."

The plague spread quickly. Anarchy broke out. Divorcing couples swapped partners with other divorcing couples. Middle-aged men drove past with twentyish girlfriends, while middle-aged women found jobs in the city and left their kids alone at home all day. So many feuds erupted, so many lines were drawn, that my parents stopped throwing parties at the house.

Two years later kids like me, the children of parents

who hadn't broken up yet, were feeling a little out of it socially. The gangs of divorced kids had an edgy glamour, while I felt like a blob of normalcy. Divorced kids smoked, both cigarettes and pot—often right at the kitchen table with their exhausted-looking single moms. The boys learned how to strike matches with one hand and taught themselves to use knives and kung fu throwing stars. They kidded the girls about "sixty-nining" and stayed up watching the *Tonight Show* on TV. What's more, these little toughs got all the breaks. When they skipped a class or cursed out a teacher, they were sent to the mild-mannered school psychologist instead of to detention with Miss Strick.

Still, I was happy my parents had stayed together (perhaps I sensed I wouldn't survive for long among the sexy, nicotine-stoked waifs). When Mom and Dad fought—about money, about their families, about my mother's desire to take a job—I prayed on my knees for their roars and shrieks to cease. When mealtime conversations grew strained, I burst into upbeat accounts of my day. If I found a parent sobbing in the garage or raving about suicide in the bathroom (not uncommon events as time went on), I would tiptoe outside and then run into the woods, where I liked to lie on the ground with my eyes shut, listening to the wind.

Finally, as if to save ourselves, we moved. My father left his position as a patent lawyer for a Fortune 500 corporation and decided to go into private practice. We packed up a U-Haul and drove to sunny Phoenix, leaving behind the gloomy northern village that had come to resemble Peyton Place. The move meant new friends, new prospects, new beginnings. On the trip down I dyed my blond hair blonder, believing new hair might render me more popular.

In Arizona my parents found God. We joined the Mormon Church. The Mormons' true gospel, we quickly learned, was family unity, family love, and many of the converts were like us: middle-class households feeling modern strains, desperate for old-time religion's sturdy clamp. Once a week, according to Mormon practice, we gathered for "family home evening" in the living room. My mom served lemonade. We prayed. Sang songs. My father read uplifting passages from books. I remember thinking we were faking it, that our newfound contentment was an act, but I also remember feeling grateful for it.

And the act seemed to work. My parents' marriage stabilized. When Phoenix's heat and urban stresses got to us, my father rejoined the corporation he'd spurned and we moved back to Minnesota, to a farm town—a community so small and isolated that divorce and chaos hadn't touched it yet. It was as if we'd traveled back in time. Fathers worked out-of-doors and mothers worked indoors and children grew up under a canopy of safety.

From this patched foundation, I took off. I got into Princeton and graduated with honors. I won a scholarship to Oxford, where I met the girl I'd later marry. We moved to New York and I found a magazine job and started writing short stories. I published a book.

For all these blessings, I felt grateful, and I still do. I also know that if my parents had split and turned my life upside down as a teenager, these wonderful things might never have come my way.

The problem is that when my parents *did* split, it felt as if none of them ever had.

AT FIRST, I reacted well to the divorce, I thought. I took my wife's position: For years my parents' marriage had been on life support, and while pulling the plug might prove painful, it was necessary. In time Mom and Dad would both be better off.

"It's not as if anyone's died," my wife reminded me, "or fallen gravely ill." My wife's mother was a paraplegic, suffering from multiple sclerosis, so these words had force. I decided that my minor family trauma just didn't warrant a big emotional breakdown, so I resolved not to have one.

It didn't work. As the conflicts between my parents heightened and multiplied, my all-consuming childhood desire to keep things smooth between them reemerged. I stepped into the cross fire. I couldn't help it. Though I no longer lived in my parents' house, it soon became clear that, emotionally, I'd never really left home.

I grew exceedingly odd that year. I'd always been a nervous, sensitive type, prone to bouts of worry and self-doubt, but now I was having trouble functioning. I stopped being able to enter stores and banks. I'd freeze at the threshold and send my wife in, convinced that the clerk or teller was mad at me. I got funny about money, too. My wife and I both had comfortable incomes, yet I nearly bit off her head one day for losing a five-dollar bill. "I *earned* that money!" Convinced that bankruptcy was truly near, I raged for hours about the incident, then fled the apartment and rode the subways all night. I imagined that I was homeless, cast adrift, and I enjoyed this thought. Later that week I went underground again, provoked by my wife's purchase of a muffin pan that I wasn't sure she really needed.

My work, strangely enough, was going well. I wrote a weekly magazine column whose readership seemed to be growing nicely, but I needed to chain-smoke and drink to get the words out. The hacking cough I developed appealed to me, much as the homeless fantasy had. The burn of straight whiskey felt vaguely comforting, too.

Naturally, my wife was growing worried. Her anxious eyes were hard for me to face. When she suggested I talk to a therapist, I agreed, but I never made the call.

Instead I talked to my dissolving family. That Dairy Queen phone call was just the first of hundreds. With me in New York, my parents in Minnesota, and my brother in Illinois, the long-distance carriers had us where they wanted us: thousands of miles apart and in crisis. Sometimes, when I put the the phone down after a marathon exchange of calls, I'd have to massage my right ear to get the feeling back.

The Kirn family built its own Internet of grief that year. We surfed the web of dysfunction. The calls flew in all directions, at all hours, crisscrossing, overlapping, and daisy-chaining. Two by two, in every combination, family members shared secrets, swore pacts, rehearsed deceptions, and blurted out confessions. The breakup was painful enough by itself, but the electronic filters made it maddening. If the divorce had happened in my youth, when the family still lived under one roof, I probably would have witnessed tearful pleas, thunderous accusations, rattling door slams. Emotions would have been attached to *scenes*. As it was, I had nothing to hold on to.

I underwent a cyber-split: an electronic, disembodied trauma. With no one to look in the eye, I grew distrustful. With no one to look in my eyes, I grew untrustworthy. I doubted others' true feelings and hid my own. Finally, I stopped listening to everyone. The divorce had made my world seem unreliable, but the phone calls had rendered it unreal. Only the calling patterns themselves held meaning for me. By interpreting busy signals, call-waiting beeps, and the behavior of various answering machines, I could figure out who was speaking to whom, who was whose enemy, and if anyone had died yet. Finally, this was all I cared to know.

Back in the physical realm, in my apartment, things were bad. My wife was staying with friends. My money tantrums, boozy workathons, and grocery-store terrors had finally gotten to her. Plus, I was feeling jealous all the time. And not bathing. And weeping at breakfast. I'd gone insane. I blamed the divorce, but deep down I knew the truth: Nothing other people had done to me could justify what I was doing to others.

The solution, I decided, was to move. Now that my childhood home was gone, the dream of buying my own house consumed me. My wife and I discussed the idea. She seemed agreeable, but wanted to wait. Her refusal to commit annoyed me. If I could only leave New York, I thought, and settle into a simpler way of life, my nerves would heal. I'd become a better husband. All I wanted was a second chance.

That month I flew to Montana to write an article on a doomsday cult near Yellowstone Park. I stayed in a sweet little town of shops and churches and tree-shaded houses and laughing kids on bikes. It reminded me of my hometown in Minnesota before the elms died. I fell into a trance. One morning, after a long night in the bars, I entered a real estate office and made an offer on a cute yellow bungalow I'd seen. The offer was accepted. My wife was shocked.

I flew back to New York and packed a gym bag, boxed up some books and sent them UPS, and moved out West alone. I'd finally snapped. I slept on the floor of my empty new house and ate Kentucky Fried Chicken for every meal. My wife, when we spoke on the phone, still talked of following me, but instead of encouraging her, I hemmed and hawed.

The fact was I was having an affair. It had started in a bar, the age-old story, and though I'd known from the start I didn't love the woman and probably never would, I couldn't leave her. Weirdly, I felt my honor was at stake. Having already cheated on one woman, my wife, I somehow felt bound to stay true to my girlfriend.

A few weeks later I told my wife about the other woman. My wife immediately asked for a divorce. Our breakup was quick and amicable and businesslike: a simple exhange of documents through the mail and the splitting down the middle of a savings account. The procedure cost less than a hundred dollars, far, far less than our wedding. *Poof! You're single.* The only snag, as I remember, was being asked to sign a piece of paper confessing to something called "Virtual Abandonment." I hesitated, offended. Then I signed.

After having ruined my marriage, I took pride in having achieved the perfect divorce. It allowed me to feel superior to my parents, who were still in court. When I phoned them to announce my own bad news, they didn't show sufficient pity, I felt. I cursed them, left the house, got drunk downtown, and passed out on some railroad tracks.

I woke the next morning hungover but thrilled. I was a divorced kid, too, now, a sexy wild outcast. I was free. I went on a spree that summer. I partied hearty. I hung out with guys who rode Harleys. I smoked fat joints. I drove a hundred miles per hour, the stereo cranked, tossing beer cans out the window. Looking at snapshots taken around that time, I'm shocked by my puffiness, my aimless gaze, the greasy sheen to my colorless, ashen skin, and yet I remember the summer as euphoric. Except for the nights when I woke up sobbing, missing my ex-wife, and the nonstop screaming matches with my girlfriend; except for the panic attacks while buying groceries and the vomiting fits in taverns' men's rooms, I was having fun!

My father came out to Montana to fish one weekend. He didn't look well. He'd lost a lot of weight. Just hours after eating lunch with him—the first time we'd seen each other in over a year—I lost control of my girlfriend's Jeep and skidded over a cliff. The vehicle rolled four times as it fell, smashing into trees and boulders. A tire iron, loose in the backseat, boomeranged past my head, breaking windows. When the Jeep came to rest upside down in a streambed, I felt cold water running through my hair and thought it was fuel. I braced for an explosion.

My bashed-up girlfriend looked at me from the passenger seat. "We're through," she said.

It was the funniest remark I'd ever heard.

I ended up in the emergency room. The doctors X-rayed me and gave me stitches, agreeing that my survival was a miracle. I got back home at five in the morning and found a single message on my machine. "Walt, it's Mom. It's very late. Please call me. I don't care when you get this, call me."

I dialed her number.

"Thank God, it's you," she said. "I woke up at eleven from a dream that you'd died in a ditch somewhere. You'd bled to death. I know it sounds terribly silly, but it seemed real."

I fingered the gauze on my lacerated forehead. "Well, as a matter of fact . . . ," I said.

THERAPY, sobriety, exercise, medication, friends, and time. Everything helps. But such comeback stories are boring. In the six years since that summer of dual divorces, I've tried every self-help program I can think of, with generally gratifying results. Something woke up in me when I smashed that Jeep. I resolved to get better, whatever better might be. I like to think I've made progress, but who knows?

The truth is that the divorces still gnaw at me. There will be no more family Christmases. I've fallen out of touch with my ex-wife. My parents' legal squabbles continue, while my brain seems irreparably divided into Mom's side and Dad's side. And the question of whether I'm thankful that my parents stayed married so long for my sake seems insoluble. Sometimes I wish they'd split when I was young and introduced me to modern chaos earlier. A lot of those teenage divorced kids I once knew

162

❑

My Parents'
Bust-Up.
And Mine.

sunk and never resurfaced, to be sure, but the ones who survived seem enviably vibrant to me. They're dynamic, open, unafraid. They front the best new rock bands, direct controversial independent movies, write visionary computer software. The road less taken is where they're most at home. Me, I'm halting, ironic—a stricken traditionalist. Institutions that those wised-up waifs dismiss outright are still appealing to me.

Such as marriage. As I write this, my second wedding is days away. Her name is Maggie, and I'll be her first husband. The ceremony will take place in a church. Maggie seems confident we'll grow old together, despite the fact her mother and father have both been married three times. I hope she's right. I dream of a lasting marriage, too, though it's hard to admit it aloud. Still, what the hell?

Love may be fated to sour and spread suffering, but what am I supposed to do about it? Crying for doomed humanity is God's job.

Me, I'm off to marry my sweetheart.

LEARNING

TO BE SINGLE

BY *Lawrence Block*

In June of 1981 I spent a couple of nights in Wesley House, a youth hostel in Iowa City. I shared a room with a fellow named Joe, who was going to be staying on in Iowa City, but not in Wesley House. He'd made arrangements to rent a room in a fraternity house for the summer, a move that would give him more space for less money. We were paying five bucks a night each to share a room at the hostel, while the single in the fraternity house would be his alone for sixty dollars a month.

I was two weeks away from my forty-third birthday. Joe was thirty-six, and his field, as far as I could make out, was speech and drama. He was originally from Rochester and had lived in Philadelphia and Houston. He was sort of drifting, he said, as a way of getting over his divorce.

"My friends say I should get back into the swing of things," he confided, "but I know I'm not ready yet."

"These things take time," I said.

"Boy, you're right about that," he said. "And you can't accelerate the process, either."

We fell silent. Then I asked him how long it had been.

"Five years," he said.

I HAD NEVER been to Iowa before, and that, really, was the principal reason why I was there now. It was one of the six states I'd not yet visited, and it was my plan to get to four of them—Iowa, North Dakota, Montana, and Idaho—before returning to New York. (Alaska and Hawaii would have to wait. Fifteen years later, remarkably enough, they're still waiting.)

Sometime in the spring I'd arranged to part company with the woman with whom I'd been living for the past three and a half years. We agreed that she would retain the apartment, while I would leave my stuff in it until I found someplace else to live.

"Relationships don't end," a friend told me. "They change." This one had changed utterly, and I felt the mixture of relief and disappointment characteristic of such an occasion.

It struck me that I was free as a bird. If I had no place to live, neither did I have any rent to pay, or any abiding reason to rush to find a place. I'd just finished a book, and was ready for some professional downtime. So why hang around? I batted out three months' worth of columns for *Writer's Digest,* crammed some clothes into a backpack, waited until a minute after midnight on

June 2 to mail my New York Marathon entry at the main post office, and walked over to the Port Authority bus terminal to catch an outbound Greyhound.

I stayed overnight at a YMCA in Columbus, Ohio, rode another Greyhound to Chicago, and stayed for almost a week at the Y on Diversey. I ran or racewalked along Lake Michigan every day, and on Sunday I ran in the ten-mile Zoo Run through Lincoln Park. I collected my T-shirt and left the next morning for Iowa City.

It was, I should mention, my year for running. I'd started jogging four years before, after a remarkably non-athletic youth, and embraced it with the passion of the late bloomer.

God knows I wasn't good at it. I was slow, and a weak knee would always force me to switch to racewalking at some point in the course of a long race. But I was obsessive, in this as in much else, and I got the job done. I ran regularly in races in New York, and already that year I had finished two full marathons, in London and Madrid. Now I was bringing along a copy of *Running Times* with a schedule of races all over the country, and planning my route accordingly. I'd left a lot of race T-shirts in the apartment that was no longer mine, and I intended to return to New York with quite a few more.

I went out for a training run my first morning in Iowa City and was surprised by the rolling hills. I'd thought the whole state was going to be flat. I was planning to run in the North Dakota marathon in Grand Forks the last weekend in June—I'd picked it because I was sure it would be flat as a fritter—but first I had a five-miler coming up in Fort Dodge, Iowa, and a 10-K in Clark, South Dakota.

I trotted along, breathed the fresh air, listened to the

birds. And thought about Joe, and the recovery he was being careful not to rush.

Five years. *Sheesh!*

I WAS NOT quite twenty-two when I got married in 1960. That seems ridiculously young now, and it even seemed young then. At the time I told myself that I was old beyond my years, an experienced fellow, a veritable man of the world. Yeah, right. It is true that I had lived away from home and that I was capable of supporting myself as a freelance writer, but so what? I was young beyond my years. I was callow to the max.

A year later my daughter was born. Two years later we had a second daughter. In our seventh year of marriage, I found myself in a spectacularly indecorous affair that wrecked a few friendships and looked to have ended my marriage. I flew over to Ireland to think about it—I have always tended to apply geographical solutions to nongeographical problems—and came back two months later to resume being married. We bought a house in the country and acquired goats, rabbits, geese, donkeys, a lamb, a pony, and a third daughter. Then, in year fourteen, I moved back to New York. Alone.

Except I wasn't alone, not really. I didn't know how to be single. I don't think I saw it as an option.

I lived by myself in New York, but I had a woman I saw three or four nights a week and spoke to daily. That went on for nine months, and then we broke up and I started a relationship with another woman, on about the same basis. (Actually, I blush to admit, there was an overlap of a couple of weeks. Then the first woman found out about the second one.)

After four or five months the new woman called it

quits. I was drinking a lot at the time, it may not astonish you to learn, and I did not take the breakup terribly well. I dated a lot, to no clear purpose. I listened, over and over again, to an album of Eydie Gorme singing torch songs.

I stopped drinking for three months and spent hours on end in my apartment, producing a hooked rug of my own design. I resumed drinking and put Eydie back on the turntable.

In January of 1975 I flew to Buffalo, where my mother and stepfather lived. I had to have surgery to remove a kidney stone wedged in the ureter. While I was mending I had a couple of dates with a woman there in Buffalo. A month or so later she came to visit me in New York, and in the spring I went up to Buffalo and stayed with her for about a month.

We decided I would move in permanently. I would clear out and give up my New York apartment, and we would live happily ever after. I bought a big old Ford wagon and drove to New York, sold off everything that wouldn't fit in it, and headed back to Buffalo. As I pulled into her driveway, she came out the door with a curious expression on her face.

"I've been thinking," she said. "I don't know if this is going to work."

"Now you tell me," I said.

A week later I loaded my stuff back in the car, stowed most of it in my mother's attic, gave the rest away, and got out of town.

NOT MUCH was clear to me, but this much was: I couldn't live anywhere. Not in Buffalo, not in New

York, not with someone, not by myself. A friend of mine was living in Los Angeles, writing movies and screenplays. I decided to go out there, but in an unhurried fashion. I set out in July, and I got there in February.

Well, what was the rush? I spent August on Fire Island with my kids, then drove down to the North Carolina Outer Banks and spent a month fishing off the pier and living on what I caught. I had a date with a recently divorced woman in Greenville, South Carolina, the friend of a friend, and I spent a few evenings with another woman in Charleston. I believe she'd been divorced, too, but not that recently. I met her at a Unitarian breakfast.

I went to Jekyll Island, Georgia, and to Saint Augustine, Florida, where I managed to get a book written. I went up to Greenville to spend Christmas, then back to Florida where my daughters joined me for New Year's.

I got to L.A. in February and got an apartment at the Magic Hotel. I wrote some, and spent time with my friend. I also dated, though I never had more than a couple of dates with the same person. In retrospect, it seems to me that most of them were stunningly inappropriate. One was a black woman who was passing as Eurasian and who must have been some kind of semipro hooker. I met her through a dating service—she'd put her name in as a lark—and I saw her three or four times. She had three different names that I knew about. I liked her, but I couldn't keep up with her.

I had a date with a woman I met at a Parents Without Partners mixer out in the Valley. I have no idea why I thought it would be a good idea to go there. I was still at the Magic Hotel in Hollywood, and I used up half a tank of gas getting there and back. I called this woman the next day and took her to a play on Saturday, a really lousy production of something by Moss Hart.

Afterwards she asked me how I liked it. I said I liked the play but not the performance, and she couldn't figure out what I meant. Wasn't it all the same thing?

It struck me that she would probably not be an ideal life companion for a writer.

ONE NIGHT while I was in L.A. I called the woman from Charleston, the Unitarian breakfast one. She'd moved, and it took a few calls to track her down. It turned out she'd gotten married less than a month after I left town.

"Well, congratulations," I said, and we exchanged a couple of awkward sentences. I felt as though I'd missed some sort of opportunity. Then I said, "Look, I'm sure you'll be very happy, but if it doesn't work out, you know how to get in touch with me."

"I'll remember that," she said.

IN JULY my daughters came to stay at the Magic Hotel with me, and in August I drove them back to New York. I'd planned on returning to California, but I wound up staying in New York. I kept finding women to spend time with.

There is a mythical bird with one wing shorter than the other, doomed by biology to fly around in ever-diminishing concentric circles. My relationships were like that, growing shorter and shorter. (The bird, according to legend, eventually flies through its own anal aperture and disappears—and I daresay the analogy holds up just fine.)

Then, in March of 1977, right around the time I stopped drinking, I met a woman with whom I seemed to hit it off. In September we found an apartment together in the Village and stayed together until I got on that Greyhound.

I EARNED T-SHIRTS in Fort Dodge and Clark. I spent a week in Fargo, taking long training runs around town, and then I went up to Grand Forks and completed my third marathon of the year. The course was as flat as I'd hoped. I moved on, through Montana and Idaho. I lingered for a week or so in Coos Bay, Oregon. I ran in a half-marathon in Cottage Grove, then rode on into California. I ran in the Gay Run in San Francisco and picked up a tank top to go with my T-shirts. I caught a last bus to L.A., stayed two weeks knocking off a quickie bit of screen writing, and spent some of the windfall profits on a plane ticket home.

I'd been gone close to three months, and this time I hadn't dated anybody, hadn't even made the effort. But I was already in my next relationship.

A couple of nights before I left New York, I'd spent the night with a former lover, a woman with whom I had a long and complicated history. I figured I'd wind up with her when I got back.

And I did. First I sublet an apartment in the Village, a dank little basement with mushrooms growing out of the walls. Two months of that and I said the hell with it and moved in with her in Washington Heights, and in less time than it takes to tell about it, I could see that this wasn't going to work out, either.

I moved in with her in November. In March I moved across the river to Brooklyn, where I found a railroad flat in the Polish section of Greenpoint.

I'd barely settled in when I found myself thinking about a woman I'd met a few months back, the producer of a theatrical revue for which I'd written several songs. I'd decided at the time to give her a call if I ever found myself back in circulation. I thought about it for a day or two and called her from a pay phone on the Upper East Side. Hi, I said. Hi, she said. Di dah di dah di dah. Had she seen *Diner* yet? She hadn't. Well, would she like to go tomorrow night? She would.

We set a time and place to meet, and I hung up the phone, and I remember the thought that went through my mind: *Well, now I suppose I'm going to have this god-damn woman around my neck for the rest of my life.*

I stood there in the street and laughed.

WHAT I BEGAN to realize, after I stopped laughing, was that the divorce I'd undergone back in 1973 still had some unfinished business attached to it. Unlike Joe, my roommate in Iowa City, I wasn't having trouble recovering from the divorce. What I couldn't seem to do was complete it.

I was still married. Oh, not to my ex-wife. Those ties were cut. But I was still wedded to the idea of being married. I had never managed to learn to be single.

I don't mean by this that I was helpless at living alone. I had occasional vestigial fears in that regard, like the time the previous spring, about a month before I got on the Greyhound. With the relationship's end imminent, I found myself ruminating on what was going to become of me. I decided I'd probably end up as one of those seedy old bachelors you were always running into in English spy novels, who never managed to get the laundry seen to. I'd never have anything to wear, I'd walk around with dirty underwear and soup stains on my shirtfront. I brooded about this for a while, feeling worse and worse about it, until I was able to remember that, in that particular relationship, *I* was the one who took care of the laundry for both of us.

I could live alone. I could keep myself fed and clothed and sheltered. But what I couldn't do was exist as a genuinely single guy. I was always either in a relationship or between relationships. I might be between relationships for months at a time, holding open auditions all the while, but that's not the same as being single.

In Greenpoint, I set about learning to be single. I put a ridiculous amount of work into that apartment, removing plaster and exposing brick, building, painting. The place was a sow's ear and I was trying to make a silk purse out of it, and while I recognized the futility of the pursuit, I went ahead with it anyway. I wanted to make the place nice, and I wanted to make it my own.

As for that woman I'd called, I took her to the movies and I saw her once or twice a week over the next several months. But I made sure I wouldn't have her around my neck for the rest of my life by not draping her in that position in the first place. I didn't see her too often, and I didn't call her all the time, and I let her know that she wasn't the only person I was seeing.

I was seeing the woman from Washington Heights, too. Once a week, sometimes twice. I didn't call her all the time, either. After a few months she decided that wasn't the sort of relationship she wanted, so we stopped seeing each other, but that didn't lead me to see more of the other woman. Once or twice a week was plenty. After all, I was a single guy now.

STILL, I FELT it was probably not a good idea to have just one person with whom I was keeping company. So I looked around, though not with a great deal of urgency, for someone else to hang out with once or twice a week.

Then one night I ran into a woman I'd known casually for about a year. We had mutual friends in the Village. We went out to hear some music and got a cup of coffee afterwards.

She was bright and beautiful and funny, and we had a couple of dates over the next couple of weeks, and one thing led to another. It was clear to both of us from the beginning that neither of us wanted to be in a relationship. She had just recently moved out on a guy she'd been living with for five years, and I, well, we know my story. She had a comfortable little apartment on Charles Street, and I had my place in Greenpoint, and we were both happy where we were. We enjoyed each other's company, and we could continue to enjoy it, but that was all it was, something to have fun with. God knows it wasn't going to lead anywhere.

We were careful, for example, never to use the *L* word. We got squared away on that early on. One time, four or five months into what would have been a relationship but for the fact that we weren't having one, we were walking hand in hand down Charles Street and she got carried away.

"I love you," she said, and we both stopped walking and stood and stared at each other, and she put her hand to her mouth.

"I'm sorry," she said. "It just slipped out. Anyway, I didn't mean it in a bad way."

Do I have to go on with this? I mean, you can see the rest coming, can't you?

In February of 1983 we got engaged, and eight months later we were married, and we have been idyllically happy ever since. There are a number of reasons why, but there is one factor I'd point to as a *sine qua non*.

See, I was ready to be married. The divorce process was complete. I'd finally learned how to be single.

BANGING THE EX

BY *Daniel Asa Rose*

Un ragoût réchauffé n'est jamais bon.
—FRENCH PROVERB

SO IT EVOLVED. After eighteen months of yearning
for the ex—of being on a writing junket in Beijing and
coming in from a banquet at 11 p.m. and seeing the
clock in the hotel lobby tell me that back in Providence
it was 11 a.m. and my ex was taking her morning exercise
class, of coming home from Rio or Cairo or Capetown
only to get hit with a whiff of her perfume when my
boys ran down her driveway to hug me—we tried a little
experiment. We hopped in the sack.

Eighteen months. You'd think that would be long
enough. And in a sense it was. I was almost OK by then.
I no longer felt sorry for myself when I took the boys
to the zoo and noted how all the monkeys acted like a

family. I'd stopped yelling "I'll get it" when the phone rang. I'd learned the number of the pizza delivery by heart. I was no longer timid on blind dates. On medical forms, I automatically named my sister instead of my ex as next of kin. I'd even forgotten how to spell her hometown of Tuscaloosa.

Now that the grisly court proceedings were behind me, I'd also learned how to hook up with a hundred press trips that took me far from the scene of the debacle we called our marriage, and thereby to fuck everything in sight. Gallivanting thusly was a defensive move, however. The notion that my ex was suddenly available to any man who happened to tickle her fancy but me was so terrifying that I had to neutralize its power by making myself even more available to women than she was to men. Only in that manner could I get any rest, and find a strange forgiveness.

Nevertheless, all of my fucking around barely covered my dark secret: deep down, I was a one-woman man. Whatever promiscuity may have meant to her—defiance, joie de vivre, whatever—it wasn't that way for me. Promiscuity for me was a form of mourning. I was grieving with my cock. I figured it this way: The world had taken away my wife and in compensation had made all women my wives. For a while it felt as if all I had to do was reach out and there one or two would be, beauty queens from remote Fijian islands, eager to help me mourn. It was as though I was hopping from honeymoon to honeymoon, when all I really wanted was my wife in our Sunday morning bed with our boys on either side. But it was never her, my Southern belle who'd gone savage. She whom I wanted most had succumbed to military rhetoric over family life, turning into a kind of Apache sado-squaw, a member of some tribe of warrior women who thought that the answer to an unhappiness they couldn't name was to scalp the men they loved. Which of course only made me more desperate to have her.

The short-range solution, I found, was to inform her on a regular basis that I hoped she rotted in hell.

But I was, as I say, almost OK; my scalp had nearly healed, leaving behind a tender blue scar that other women seemed attracted to. Mesmerized, they breathed on it; a few even kissed it. They were respectful of its power, but not unduly so—as though they had encountered such wounds before and recognized that it had been made by one of their own.

I was almost OK, then, even though I still counted my divorce in terms of months, like a new parent counting how long it has been since the child was born. The children themselves were doing well. The six-year-old was chattering up a storm, storing away a million questions to ask me when we were together. The baby was beginning to sound out a few words and it was questionable how much he understood about the way things used to be. Women I dated were crazy about them both—the custom we had of kissing the meat loaf we all three constructed before we put it in the oven, and how adorable they looked trudging in front of us on our winter walks. When I'd ask if we were on the right path for home, they'd shrug all bundled up, their shoulders rising in their little snowsuits.

It was they who kept me on track. Throughout my wild heroic desperate promiscuity, while I was dancing out there by myself amid all those women, isolated as only a divorced person is and fucking up a storm, linking and breaking, linking and breaking, my boys were my only constant. All those nights driving home in a fog so thick I couldn't see a thing but the stuffing of gray porous cardboard beyond my headlights, there they were, my center, somewhere out in the fog, twin lighthouse beams to guide me home.

As for my ex, from the get-go she never admitted that she was anything less than OK. Whatever hurt or confusion she felt she kept hidden beneath an attitude of blithe and impenetrable cheeriness. It reminded me of the term in nineteenth-century medical literature for the bemused unconcern some people use to deny psychological pain—"*la belle indifference.*" "What's the big deal?" she would ask, genially, when I tried to talk to her. "People move out on people all the time. Why are you getting so hot and bothered?"

Grinning a great big scared grin, and not troubling to explain what she was doing except to mouth the party line that she owed it to herself to be free, she had gone out and bought a mansion from which the boys' voices, over the phone, always echoed. Even though she had filled it up with new toys for them, gourmet foods, nannies coming, housekeepers going, decorators reupholstering chairs, and designers paint-speckling floors, still it managed to echo with emptiness. The boys lived with her on weekdays, and when I wasn't off screwing the planet, I had them weekends. The rest of the time I lived alone, with enough evidence of them—an alarm clock in the ice bucket, rubber snakes in my sneakers—to remind me that I didn't really live alone.

But although my ex never *saw* me anymore—she had

turned me into a ghost as I had turned her into a witch—still there remained a presumption of intimacy between us that sputtered and threw sparks. I noticed, for instance, that when she sat beside me at a piano recital for our older son, she clapped in time with me. Unconsciously, she was still involved in my rhythms. She even stopped clapping the instant I did, as though taking her cues from me in a way she never did when we were married. Was this a kind of flirting?

Clearly what was about to transpire was in a sense unavoidable. But then again, a woman once told me that if I were an Apache, myself, my name would be "Plays With Fire." In that sense, then, anything dangerous was unavoidable.

So this night I got home from a date at eleven-thirty to find a message on my answering machine from my ex asking me to call her. I did, and found her in a state of high anxiety: She suspected the baby's nanny had been stealing from her. It was an awful situation, she said, because this latest nanny was so good with the baby and he loved her—but what could she do if the woman was stealing?

"She's a klepto, really. You ought to see what she's got stashed in her room from God knows where."

"Is she there now?"

"It's her night off. She'll be back first thing in the morning. It's so scary, to be living with someone you think you know . . ."

I bit my tongue.

"Could you come have a look?"

I was flattered enough to be needed—didn't she employ someone who could fill this job detail?—that I agreed. I put some snapshots of the boys that I'd been meaning to give her in my wallet and I drove fast over to her house, half eager to get there and half hoping to crash on the wet leaves. In a few minutes I had parked my car around the corner and was walking to her door. The lights of the city were on, and all those stars, doing what they do. It was autumn suddenly! I took a sip from my flask, ran my hand over my hairline, and rang the bell.

"I'm very upset," said my ex with a scared grin, swinging open the heavy oak door. She was wearing a flannel nightgown with the neck buttons misaligned.

The house was gigantic and mysterious to me, almost Kremlinlike in its off-limitedness. There were few places in the world as off-limits to me as the interior of this fortress, which always smelled like burnt sugar, like something delicious that had been ruined or like something that tasted great but was bad for you.

Though it was nearly midnight, our older boy had padded out of his bedroom in his footsie pajamas and was leaning over the balustrade upstairs, as frolicsome as if it were noon. "Hey Dad, can you teach me how to tie a tie?"

"Go back to sleep, loverboy."

"But Dad, do you make root beer out of roots? Why do people always faint backwards? Come see my new puppy!"

For sure enough, he was accompanied by a Dalmatian puppy as frolicsome as he was, scrabbling its nails on the shiny parquet floor but not getting enough traction, and falling on its chin and scrabbling some more.

"He's very nice but don't wake your little brother. It would be confusing to see me here."

"It's not confusing, it's nice!" he said, smiling to me

as he and the dog went slipping and sliding back into his room.

I must say, it *was* nice. The idea of being here all together, as natural as a family of monkeys, was so nice it hurt. It made me wince to think how great it would be to be able to bounce a basketball on my ex's driveway with my sons on a school night.

"You have any salad?" I asked her.

"Are you hungry?"

"I don't know what I am," I said.

With a ferret gleam in her eye, my ex led me up the stairs to the nanny's quarters on the third floor to show me what a klepto the woman was: the 120 boxes of Magic Markers, the closet full of soup cans, the stacks of neatly packaged watchbands. Standing boldly close with a nervous little smile flickering on her lips, she asked in a voice both helpless and coquettish: "What should I do?"

"Fire her."

"But not till I have a replacement, certainly."

I had nothing to say to this. Replacements were a tricky subject, given all the lovers each of us had had since our breakup.

"It's so frightening," she said. "When someone you trust betrays you, you think the world is going crazy."

I felt forlorn, standing there with her in such a familiar yet foreign way. I avoided looking at her because it pained me to see what I'd lost, up close. She had such an aura of cool beauty, of unreachable ex-ness, that it made my heart sting. I longed for her, ten inches away. She was everything I could never have in my life: cheerleaders who wanted to date only the football team, a

Lionel train set I'd yearned for when I was a kid, penny stocks that had skyrocketed in value after I'd sold them, everything in the world I had ever lost or that had been taken from me.

I mumbled something to myself.

"What?" she said.

"Nothing," I said.

"But you said something. What was that, a Pink Floyd lyric?"

"It's a poem by Swinburne," I said. "She hath wasted the something of something."

"Well, are you going to recite it?"

"That's all I remember."

Smiling, she led the way across the hall to her study and pointed out how nice it would be when the new sconces were in. The house was full of colorful paint chips taped to the walls, drapery swatches, carpet samples—so much enthusiasm. Her eyes still had that ferret gleam, and maybe mine did, too, by now, for I could see that her blood had regained the capacity to be roused by me. She wore a flush high on her cheeks as she stood studying the muscles in my neck. I could tell she was remembering what it was like to sleep with me, and was calculating what it would cost to do so again. We were excited, but we were also scared and suspicious to be standing there like this. It felt illegal. It felt like the teachers were gone and we could do whatever we wanted. I was something that had blown in from the night and wasn't supposed to be there: a train robber, maybe. Or an alien, horny and sad.

Wanting nothing more than to fix those nightgown buttons of hers, I said: "I'm sorry I told you I hope you rot in hell. Actually that's the last thing I want, but I don't know what to do with all the feelings I have toward you."

Keeping her gaze from my face, she let her head drop to my shoulder in a gesture of semisurrender, and said with peculiar wistfulness, "Oh what are we going to do?"

It was as though we'd had a long fight, as though she'd been hitting me and was exhausted and I'd been hitting her and was exhausted, and just as we were about ready to hit each other again, I took her chin in my hand and kissed her instead.

"I really loved you," I said softly. "I guess that's all I'm trying to say."

"I never loved anyone but you," she said.

Hearing this was so startling that I let a moan slide from my throat. "I dreamed—," I said, but she found my eyes, then, and for the first time in eighteen months she *saw* me, and she was kissing my mouth, and then kissing my hair, and we were crying in each other's hair, trying not to let the other know we were crying.

And when I opened my arms she fit right in. We hugged for a long time. We went to her bedroom, which smelled like the source of burnt sugar, forbidden and raw. Sitting on her bed I took out my flask and gave us both a belt of Scotch. Then it was my turn to grin, as I moved forward.

(I remember these nipples . . . you spoiled me rotten in bed . . . did we used to do it this way . . . oh why did we ever stop . . .)

And there was the aroma again that you wouldn't think would come out of all those fancy soaps and expensive linens and designer clothes and deb balls. When we were first married I used to think of her smell as the smell of Southern lake water, piney and pure, and so clear that if you skipped a pebble in the morning, you could swim out that afternoon and still see it lying at the bottom. "Fresh as a prep school girl," I used to say. But toward the end her smell had gotten more interesting. It had some grit to it, a smell out of the Alabama River mud—gambling on the river, flash of an oil spill, tang of an orange peel, a water rat darting past, and fish so frightened they were mean. It made me want to fuck her more.

(I miss this . . . it's all coming back to me . . . I never thought we'd . . . oh, do that again . . .)

Eighteen months, and it happened because I was almost OK. It couldn't have happened when I was not at all OK, and it wouldn't have happened when I was entirely OK. As for her, did this mean she was truly OK or more damaged than I even suspected?

She was *seeing* me, and all the things I could never have again were encompassed in the armful that was her: cheerleaders and penny stocks and Lionel trains, and all that intercontinental yearning was mine again, too, to put to rest in triumph—that lusting from lifeless hotel lobbies in China filled with orange dust that had blown in from the Gobi Desert, from a ferry at the bottom of New Zealand, from a hippie hotel off the beach in Goa. Here it all was again and I made the most of it as she made the most of me, clapping our hands in time . . .

We solved each other's yearnings. It was curative to have that moment again, that hanging instant when she was about to come any second, poised there on the roof of the world with the wind suddenly dropped, trembling, drippy, breathless, the bells far off—like lying by railroad tracks as they begin to tremble, feeling a freight train approach from five miles away.

And when it was over, there was closure. It was not confusing. What had been confusing was that she ever stopped loving me in the first place.

But later, in my sleep, it was very confusing. We were two human beings who had sicced mad-dog lawyers on each other, after all. We had deposed each other under oath. What visions are loosed when one sleeps in the arms of a woman who keeps most of your scalp in her jewelry box? All night, dreams spun like dirty plates in my mind.

I was living alone in my childhood home with all the furniture gone . . . falling out of an airplane . . . drinking from a dog's water bowl . . . wriggling in the white satin of a coffin so I wouldn't have to spend eternity on a seam . . .

Dreaming these dreams, I felt so deeply wronged it was as if my blood cells were infused with venom and I didn't know how to keep the venom from blackening my teeth one by one . . .

And then in my sleep the poem came back to me, as fresh as the day Swinburne wrote it:

*She hath hidden and marred and made sad
The fair limbs of the Loves, the fair faces
Of gods that were goodly and glad.
She slays, and her hands are not bloody;
She moves as a moon in the wane,
White-robed, and thy raiment is ruddy,
Our lady of Pain.*

IN THE MORNING we woke on opposite sides of the bed. With one look we could both tell. I was a ghost.

She was a witch. Worst of all, *la belle indifférence* was back, coated in rhetoric.

"You took advantage of me when I was weak."

I rubbed my eyes. "What are you talking about?"

"Last night. You couldn't stand my being independent. You misjudged my needing your help for needing you. You never understood me."

"You're insane."

"See, that proves you don't take me seriously."

"Oh, I take you seriously all right, I just think you're insane."

And then the phone rang; it was her accountant. She wrapped her nightgown around her tightly and gave me a little preoccupied wave good-bye.

"In that case I'm going to Bangkok tomorrow," I announced, and I wasn't even angry because how can you be angry at a savage? I was just sadder than hell because I was wasting my life suffering for her when there were women out there who were lovely and deep and maybe even true.

And then she shot me an irritated little look like, "What, still here?"

In a nightmare rush I took the snapshots of our boys out of my wallet and threw them at her face. She screamed for me to leave. I shoved her out of bed and she hurled the phone at me and it landed on the little Dalmatian pup which had just clambered into the room with our son who was somewhere behind carrying one sock and crying, "I can't find the other one." The pup was yelping and the accountant was making little squawking noises from the floor and as I rushed out our son was sending me a look I'd never seen before, his eyes spiraling with fear and hate. I went to get my car,

187

❏

by

DANIEL
ASA ROSE

and in a moment I was driving past the house and there was the baby high on the porch in the arms of his nanny. I slowed down and saw him blinking in confusion, back and forth from her to me, sounding out the word *Car?* as he tried to understand what I was doing there. And as I coasted away I thought, Oh my God, this is going to be his first memory: *I was two years old, I was in a huge empty house, my dad was driving away in a white car, he had sunglasses on and the wind was blowing leaves down everywhere, I was in the grip of some nanny and she was waving my arm bye-bye, bye-bye, bye-bye...*

ABOUT
THE CONTRIBUTORS

LAWRENCE BLOCK'S crime fiction ranges from the urban noir of Matthew Scudder (*A Long Line of Dead Men*) to the urbane effervescence of Bernie Rhodenbarr (*The Burglar Who Thought He Was Bogart*). He lives in New York.

HERB BOYD is an award-winning journalist and author. Among his several books are *Brotherman: The Odyssey of Black Men in America—An Anthology,* edited with Robert Allen, and *Down the Glory Road,* a history of black Americans. He also has compiled an encyclopedia of black intellectuals that is scheduled for publication by Facts on File in 1997.

BENJAMIN H. CHEEVER is the author of two novels, *The Plagiarist* and *The Partisan.* He edited *The Letters of John Cheever,* and wrote the introduction to his father's journals. He has written for the *New Yorker,* the *New York Times,* the *Nation, Details, Lear's, Reader's Digest,* and the *Ladies' Home Journal.* Which proves either that he's extremely versatile, or has the backbone of a chocolate eclair. He's now working on a book of nonfiction to be titled *Square One* and published by the Free Press. He lives in upstate New York with his wife, the film critic Janet Maslin, and their two sons.

STEPHEN DOBYNS has published nine volumes of poetry, eighteen novels, and a book of essays. His most recent book of poetry, *Common Carnage,* was published by Penguin in 1996. A collection of his essays on poetry, *Best Words, Best Order,* was recently published by St. Martin's. His most recent novel is *The Church of Dead Girls* and will be put out by Henry Holt in 1997. He lives in Watertown, Massachusetts, with his wife and three children.

RICHARD GILMAN teaches at the Yale School of Drama. His books include *The Making of Modern Drama, Decadence,* and, most recently, *Chekhov's Plays, an Opening into Eternity.*

EDWARD HOAGLAND is the author of fifteen books, five of them works of fiction, in a career dating back to the middle 1950s. A native New Yorker, he has traveled widely and now lives in Vermont. His titles include *Notes from the Century Before, The Courage of Turtles, Heart's Desire, Balancing Acts,* and *African Calliope.*

WALTER KIRN is the author of *My Hard Bargain,* a collection of short stories, and *She Needed Me,* a novel.

TIM PARKS was born in Manchester, England, in 1954 and studied in the United States before moving permanently to Italy in 1980. He is the author of a number of novels, most notably *Goodness and Shear*, as well as two nonfiction accounts of life in Italy, *Italian Neighbours* and *An Italian Education*, both best-sellers. Remarkably, he still lives with his first wife and their three children.

About
the
Contributors

LUIS J. RODRIGUEZ is the author of several books, including *Always Running: La Vida Loca, Gang Days in L.A.* He is also a leading activist for urban peace. Born on the Mexican–U.S. border and raised in Los Angeles, he currently lives in Chicago with his family.

DANIEL ASA ROSE is the O. Henry prize–winning author of *Flipping for It* (a novel) and *Small Family with Rooster* (a short story collection). His essays, stories, reviews, travel and humor pieces have appeared in the *New Yorker, Esquire, GQ, Vanity Fair, Playboy*, the *New York Times Magazine*, and others. He is married to the literary agent Shelley Roth and is writing a book about an odyssey he made with his sons.

JONATHAN ROSEN'S first novel, *Eve's Apple*, will be published by Random House in the spring of 1997. His essays have appeared in the *New York Times Book Review*, the *New York Times Magazine*, and *Vanity Fair*. A long critique of the Holocaust museum in Washington, "The Trivialization of Tragedy," was included last year in *Dumbing Down: The Strip Mining of American Culture*, published by Norton. He is Associate Editor of the *Forward*, for which he created the Arts & Letters section.

MICHAEL RYAN'S autobiography, *Secret Life,* was published by Pantheon in 1995 and Vintage in 1996. His first book of poems won the Yale Series of Younger Poets Award and was nominated for a National Book Award in 1974. *God Hunger,* published by Viking, won the Lenore Marshall/*The Nation* Award for the most outstanding book of poems published in 1989. He is Professor of English in the MFA Writing Program at the University of California, Irvine.

TED SOLOTAROFF has recently completed the first volume of an autobiography, *The Truth Comes in Blows.* He lives happily with his wife of fifteen years in East Quogue, New York.

MICHAEL VENTURA'S biweekly column, "Letters at 3 A.M.," is written for the *Austin Chronicle.* His latest book is a novel, *The Death of Frank Sinatra,* published by Holt.

JOHN A. WILLIAMS is the author of several novels, among them *The Man Who Cried I Am, Captain Blackman,* and *!Click Song.* His nonfiction books include *The King God Didn't Save: Martin Luther King, Jr.* and *If I Stop I'll Die: The Comedy and Tragedy of Richard Pryor.* Williams lives in New Jersey with his second wife. They have three sons and four grandchildren. An opera, *Vanqui,* for which he did the libretto, working with composer Leslie Burrs, will premiere in 1997.